Zero Point
Weight Loss
Cookbook for Beginners

Easy & Delicious Zero Point Weight Loss Recipes That Keep You Satisfied and on Track | Enjoy Guilt-Free Flavors | Say Goodbye to Calories Counting

Yolanda Ferry

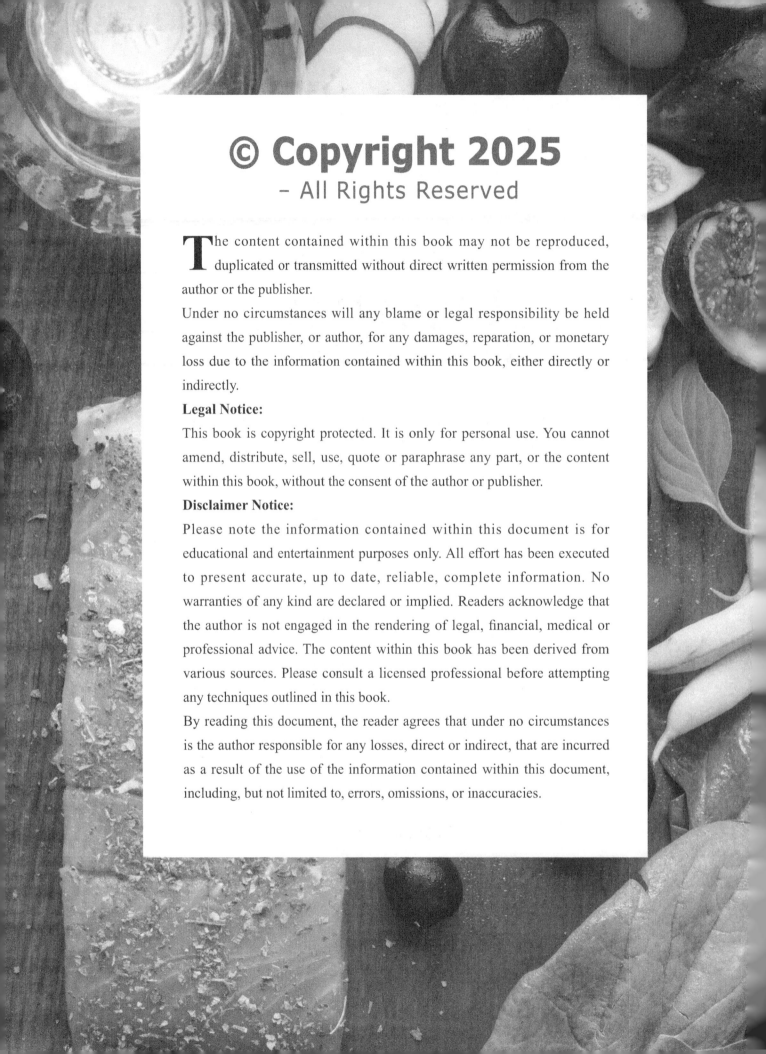

CONTENTS

Introduction

Welcome to the ultimate guide to transforming your relationship with food and achieving lasting weight loss with ease! The Zero Point Weight Loss Cookbook for Beginners is designed to simplify your journey by introducing you to the revolutionary concept of zero point foods. These foods are not only nutritious but also satisfy hunger, allowing you to enjoy eating without the hassle of calorie counting or strict portion controls.

This cookbook is packed with an impressive variety of recipes to suit every palate and lifestyle. Whether you're a busy professional looking for quick breakfast options, a parent planning wholesome family meals, or someone with a sweet tooth craving healthier desserts, there's something here for everyone. From vibrant salads and hearty soups to indulgent yet guilt-free snacks, these recipes prove that healthy eating can be both satisfying and enjoyable.

What sets this cookbook apart is its focus on simplicity and accessibility. You'll find step-by-step instructions and readily available ingredients that ensure every recipe is beginner-friendly. Plus, with clear categorization of meals—from protein-packed dinners to refreshing snacks—you can easily plan your meals for the day or week.

This book doesn't just stop at recipes. You'll also gain insights into the science behind zero point foods, helpful meal plans, and tips for adopting a sustainable, healthy lifestyle. Whether you're looking to shed a few pounds, maintain a balanced diet, or simply explore new and exciting dishes, this cookbook is your go-to resource.

Embark on your zero point weight loss journey today. With this cookbook as your guide, you'll discover that healthy eating is not only attainable but also incredibly delicious!

The Fundamentals of Zero Point Weight Loss

What is Zero Point Weight Loss?

Zero Point Weight Loss is a groundbreaking approach to healthy living, designed to simplify weight management by focusing on a specific set of zero point foods. These foods are so nutritionally robust and low in calories that you can enjoy them without needing to measure, track, or count points. By encouraging consumption of these wholesome options—like fruits, vegetables, lean proteins, legumes, and whole grains—Zero Point Weight Loss promotes healthy, mindful eating without the stress of traditional dieting.

Unlike restrictive meal plans, this approach empowers you to build plates with an abundance of satisfying and nutrient-dense foods. Whether your goal is weight loss, maintenance, or simply better eating habits, Zero Point Weight Loss provides the tools to create a sustainable and balanced lifestyle.

The Scientific Basis of Zero Point Foods

Zero Point foods are carefully selected based on their nutritional benefits, their ability to curb hunger, and their role in promoting overall well-being. Here's the science that makes them effective:

Low Energy Density: Foods like leafy greens and non-starchy vegetables have low calories per gram but high water and fiber content, allowing you to eat more while consuming fewer calories.

High Fiber Content: Foods such as legumes, whole grains, and certain fruits are packed with fiber, which helps regulate digestion, control blood sugar, and keep you full for longer periods.

Protein Powerhouse: Lean proteins like chicken breast, fish, and eggs are metabolically beneficial, helping to maintain muscle mass while boosting your calorie-burning capacity.

Natural Nutrients: Zero Point foods are typically minimally processed, providing essential vitamins, minerals, and antioxidants that support immunity, brain health, and energy levels.

Satiety and Satisfaction: By focusing on foods that take longer to digest, Zero Point Weight Loss naturally reduces cravings and the likelihood of overeating.

The Benefits of Zero Point Weight Loss

Simplifies Eating: Forget calorie counting and food scales. Focus on zero point foods to take the guesswork out of meal prep.

Supports Healthy Choices: Encourages the consumption of natural, whole, and minimally processed foods that nourish the body.

Fosters Satiety: Helps you feel satisfied with high-volume, nutrient-dense foods, reducing the likelihood of snacking or binge eating.

Customizable for All Lifestyles: Whether you're vegetarian, gluten-free, or have specific preferences, the plan is adaptable to fit your needs.

Encourages Sustainable Results: Builds healthy habits over time, promoting long-term weight maintenance rather than quick, unsustainable fixes.

Improves Overall Well-Being: Boosts energy, supports heart health, and reduces the risk of chronic diseases through a nutrient-rich eating style.

How to Get Started with Zero Point Weight Loss?

1. Learn About Zero Point Foods: Familiarize yourself with the comprehensive food list. These include categories like fruits, vegetables, lean proteins, legumes, and certain whole grains.

2. Stock Your Kitchen: Set yourself up for success by keeping your pantry, fridge, and freezer stocked with zero point staples like beans, quinoa, canned tomatoes, fresh greens, and frozen vegetables.

3. Plan Balanced Meals: Start with zero point foods as the foundation of every meal. Pair non-starchy vegetables with lean proteins and incorporate legumes or whole grains for variety.

4. Experiment with Recipes: Explore a wide range of delicious recipes like Moroccan Vegetable Tagine, Greek Chickpea Salad, or Lemon Cod with Tabbouleh. The Zero Point Weight Loss cookbook

offers endless inspiration to keep your meals exciting and satisfying.

5. Adopt Mindful Eating Practices: Slow down and savor your meals. Pay attention to hunger and fullness cues, and eat only until you feel satisfied.

6. Track Progress Without Stress: While you don't need to count points or calories, consider journaling your meals to understand what works best for you and to stay motivated.

Zero Point Cooking Tips and Tricks

Master the art of cooking with zero point ingredients and create delicious, satisfying meals with these helpful tips and tricks:

1. Flavor Boosters Without Calories

Use Fresh Herbs: Add brightness with fresh herbs like cilantro, basil, parsley, or dill.

Spices for Depth: Experiment with cumin, smoked paprika, turmeric, and chili powder to create complex flavor profiles.

Citrus Magic: A squeeze of fresh lemon or lime juice adds acidity and elevates the taste of any dish.

Vinegar Variations: Incorporate balsamic, apple cider, or red wine vinegar for a tangy twist in dressings and marinades.

2. Texture Hacks

Creamy Without Cream: Blend cooked cauliflower, Greek yogurt, or silken tofu for creamy soups, sauces, or dressings.

Crispy Snacks: Roast chickpeas or air-pop popcorn for a crunchy, zero point snack.

Layering Vegetables: Use spiralised zucchini, cauliflower rice, or shredded cabbage as a base for bowls and stir-fries to add volume.

3. Smart Cooking Techniques

Roasting for Richness: Roast vegetables like carrots, zucchini, and tomatoes to intensify their natural sweetness.

Sautéing Without Oil: Use nonstick pans or a splash of broth to sauté vegetables without adding extra calories.

Pressure Cooking: Use an Instant Pot or pressure cooker to prepare beans, lentils, and soups quickly and efficiently.

4. Meal Prepping Made Easy

Batch Cooking: Prepare large quantities of roasted vegetables, quinoa, or chickpeas to use in multiple meals.

Mason Jar Meals: Layer salads or overnight oats in mason jars for grab-and-go options.

Freeze Leftovers: Store soups, stews, and sauces in individual portions for easy reheating.

5. Creative Substitutions

Swap Oil for Broth: Replace cooking oil with vegetable or chicken broth when sautéing.

Use Cauliflower: Sub cauliflower for rice or mashed potatoes in traditional recipes.

Greek Yogurt: Substitute nonfat Greek yogurt for sour cream, cream cheese, or mayonnaise in dips and dressings.

6. Highlight Natural Sweetness

Caramelized Fruits: Grill or roast fruits like peaches, pineapple, or apples to bring out their natural sugars.

Unsweetened Cocoa: Use a touch of cocoa powder to add richness to desserts without added sugar.

Blended Fruits: Create purees with bananas or berries as a sweet base for smoothies or frozen treats.

7. Zero Point Meal Building

Balance Flavors: Combine sweet, salty, tangy, and spicy elements for a well-rounded dish.

Layer Ingredients: Start with greens, add grains or beans, top with protein, and finish with fresh herbs and a citrus-based dressing.

Experiment: Mix and match zero point foods to keep meals interesting and diverse.

8. Hydration While Cooking

Infused Water: Keep hydrated with water infused with cucumber, mint, or lemon slices.

Broth Beverages: Sip warm vegetable or chicken broth as a comforting zero point drink while preparing meals.

By incorporating these tips and tricks, you'll transform simple zero point ingredients into flavorful, satisfying dishes that keep you on track and excited about your meals.

Maintaining Long-Term Success

Zero Point Weight Loss is more than just a meal plan; it's a lifestyle transformation. To maintain your results, focus on consistency, celebrate progress, and continually adapt your approach to fit your changing needs. Here's how to stay on track:

1. Make It a Habit: Incorporate zero point foods into your daily routine until they become second nature.

2. Stay Inspired: Try new recipes, experiment with flavors, and involve friends and family in your healthy eating journey.

3. Balance and Flexibility: While zero point foods provide the foundation, occasional indulgences are fine. Just enjoy them mindfully.

4. Reflect and Adjust: Regularly evaluate your goals and adjust your plan as needed to stay motivated and on target.

Start your zero point weight loss journey today! with zero point weight loss, you'll gain a new perspective on food that prioritizes abundance, nourishment, and simplicity. say goodbye to the stress of dieting and hello to a healthier, happier you!

At the same time, the cookbook offers 5 exclusive bonuses for you to discover! The five exclusive bonuses will not only boost the value of the Zero Point Weight Loss Cookbook for Beginners, but also enhance your journey toward healthier eating:

Ingredient Substitution Guide

This guide is designed to help you substitute ingredients effectively while maintaining the principles of Zero Point Weight Loss. Whether you're looking to adapt a recipe to suit your preferences, dietary restrictions, or pantry inventory, this resource offers practical swaps for common ingredients without adding points to your meals.

1. Fruits

Sweeteners in Baking: Replace sugar with mashed bananas or unsweetened applesauce. These add natural sweetness while keeping recipes zero point.

Juice Alternatives: Instead of fruit juice, use fresh orange, lime, or lemon zest for tangy flavor without the extra points.

High-Sugar Fruits: Swap higher-sugar fruits (like mangoes) with berries such as strawberries, blueberries, or raspberries.

2. Vegetables

Pasta: Substitute regular pasta with spiralised zucchini, spaghetti squash, or julienned carrots.

Potatoes: Replace mashed potatoes with mashed cauliflower or turnips for a creamy, zero point alternative.

Starchy Vegetables: Swap corn or peas with non-starchy options like broccoli, green beans, or bell peppers.

3. Proteins

Ground Meat: Use ground turkey or chicken breast instead of beef or pork to keep recipes lean and zero point.

Breaded Proteins: Instead of breaded chicken or fish, coat them with crushed zero point crackers or bake them without breading.

Egg Replacements: Replace whole eggs with egg whites or use a zero point egg substitute for recipes like omelettes or frittatas.

4. Legumes and Beans

Chickpeas or Lentils: Swap out higher-fat protein options for legumes in soups, stews, and salads.

Refried Beans: Use whole black beans or kidney beans instead of traditional refried beans to reduce added fats.

5. Dairy

Cream or Half-and-Half: Substitute with nonfat Greek yogurt or unsweetened almond milk to achieve a creamy texture in soups or sauces.

Cheese: Use reduced-fat cottage cheese or nonfat ricotta in place of higher-fat cheeses.

Butter: Replace butter with a blend of mashed avocado or applesauce in baking, or use cooking sprays for sautéing.

6. Grains

White Rice: Replace with riced cauliflower or whole grains like farro or quinoa (check portions for zero point allowance).

Bread Crumbs: Use crushed zero point crackers or whole-grain breadcrumbs.

Flour: Substitute whole wheat flour with oat flour (made from blending oats), depending on the recipe.

7. Fats and Oils

Cooking Oils: Replace oil with cooking sprays or water sautéing. For roasting, lightly coat vegetables with broth.

Salad Dressings: Use a blend of vinegar, Dijon mustard, and fresh herbs instead of store-bought dressings.

8. Condiments and Flavorings

Sugar: Swap sugar with natural zero point sweeteners like stevia or monk fruit.

Ketchup: Replace with homemade tomato purée seasoned with garlic and vinegar.

Mayonnaise: Use nonfat plain Greek yogurt as a creamy alternative for dips and spreads.

9. Snacks

Chips: Replace potato chips with roasted chickpeas or air-popped popcorn.

Dips: Substitute sour cream-based dips with hummus or nonfat Greek yogurt mixed with herbs.

10. Baking

Flour: Use blended oats or almond meal for baking recipes.

Sweeteners: Substitute refined sugar with unsweetened applesauce, mashed bananas, or natural zero-calorie sweeteners.

Butter/Oil: Replace with applesauce, mashed pumpkin, or nonfat Greek yogurt to maintain moisture.

11. Beverages

Juice: Replace fruit juice with infusions of lemon, lime, or berries in water.

Creamer: Swap coffee creamer with unsweetened almond milk or coconut milk.

Alcohol: Replace cocktails with sparkling water infused with fresh fruit slices or herbs.

Tips for Successful Substitutions:

Taste Test: Adjust seasonings or sweeteners gradually to suit your palate when using substitutes.

Texture Adjustments: Be mindful that some swaps (like yogurt for oil) may change the texture, especially in baked goods.

Balance Nutrients: Ensure you're incorporating balanced ingredients like lean proteins, vegetables, and legumes to create satisfying zero point meals.

This guide empowers you to adapt recipes creatively while staying aligned with Zero Point Weight Loss principles.

Zero Point Food Directory

This comprehensive directory is an invaluable resource for anyone embarking on a Zero Point Weight Loss journey. From fiber-packed vegetables and fruits to lean proteins and whole grains, the directory covers all food that meet the criteria of zero point, empowering you to make informed choices. Whether you're creating recipes, dining out, or shopping for groceries, this guide eliminates guesswork, helping you stay on track effortlessly while fostering a balanced and sustainable eating lifestyle.

1. Beans, Peas & Lentils

Beans, peas, and lentils are nutrient-dense powerhouses rich in protein, fiber, and complex carbohydrates. They are excellent for promoting satiety and stabilizing blood sugar levels, making them ideal for weight management and heart health.

Whole Beans: Adzuki beans, Black beans, Kidney beans, Pinto beans, Navy beans, Great Northern beans, Cannellini beans

Peas: Green peas, Black-eyed peas, Split peas

Lentils: French green lentils, Red lentils, Brown lentils

Specialty Beans: Edamame, Lupini beans, Fava beans

Canned Options: Fat-free refried beans, Chickpeas, Soybeans

2. Chicken & Turkey Breast

Lean poultry provides high-quality protein with minimal fat content, supporting muscle maintenance and repair. It is versatile and works in countless dishes, from grilled to baked recipes.

Whole Cuts: Skinless chicken breast, Skinless turkey breast

Ground Options: Ground chicken breast, Ground turkey breast (98% fat-free)

3. Corn & Popcorn

Corn is a natural source of energy and fiber, while air-popped popcorn is a whole grain, perfect for guilt-free snacking.

Fresh Corn: Corn on the cob, Fresh sweet corn (yellow or white)

Canned Options: Canned corn, Hominy

Popcorn: Air-popped popcorn (plain, salted, or spiced without butter)

4. Eggs

Eggs are a nutrient-dense source of high-quality protein and essential vitamins. They support muscle growth, eye health, and brain function.

Whole Eggs: Fresh whole eggs, Hard-boiled eggs, Soft-boiled eggs

Egg Whites: Liquid egg whites, Scrambled egg whites (fat-free)

Egg Yolks: For nutrient-rich recipes

5. Fish & Shellfish

Fish and shellfish provide lean protein, omega-3 fatty acids, and essential minerals, supporting brain, heart, and joint health.

Fresh Fish: Salmon, Cod, Tuna, Trout, Halibut, Mackerel

Canned Options: Tuna in water, Sardines in water

Shellfish: Shrimp, Scallops, Crab, Lobster, Mussels

Specialty Items: Sashimi, Sea urchin, Smoked salmon, Anchovies in water

6. Fruits

Fruits are naturally sweet and hydrating, rich in vitamins, antioxidants, and fiber, promoting digestion, immunity, and overall wellness.

Citrus Fruits: Oranges, Lemons, Grapefruits, Limes, Clementines

Berries: Strawberries, Blueberries, Blackberries, Raspberries

Tropical Fruits: Mangoes, Papayas, Pineapples

Stone Fruits: Peaches, Plums, Apricots

Melons: Watermelon, Cantaloupe, Honeydew

Miscellaneous: Apples, Bananas, Kiwis, Pears

7. Non-Starchy Vegetables

Vegetables are the cornerstone of zero point foods. They are packed with fiber, vitamins, and minerals while being low in calories, promoting fullness and overall health.

Leafy Greens: Spinach, Kale, Romaine, Swiss chard, Collard greens

Cruciferous Veggies: Broccoli, Cauliflower, Brussels sprouts, Cabbage

Roots & Squash: Carrots, Beets, Butternut squash, Pumpkin

Alliums: Onions, Garlic, Leeks, Shallots

Others: Zucchini, Eggplant, Okra, Mushrooms, Peppers

8. Tofu & Tempeh

Tofu and tempeh are plant-based protein sources loaded with iron and calcium, supporting bone health and muscle recovery.

Firm Tofu: Ideal for grilling or stir-frying

Soft & Silken Tofu: Great for soups, desserts, and smoothies

Tempeh: A nutrient-rich fermented soybean product

9. Dairy and Dairy Alternatives

These options deliver protein, calcium, and essential nutrients while maintaining low calorie and fat content.

Plain nonfat Greek yogurt: High in protein and probiotics for gut health.

Plain nonfat cottage cheese: Excellent for muscle recovery with a mild taste.

Plant-Based Options: Almond yogurt, Soy yogurt, Quark (up to 1% fat)

Unsweetened almond milk (without added sweeteners): Low-calorie alternative rich in vitamin E.

10. Whole Grains

Certain whole grains are zero points due to their fiber and nutrient density, especially when minimally processed. These grains promote satiety, digestive health, and sustained energy.

Quinoa: Complete protein and rich in essential amino acids.

Bulgur: High in fiber and promotes digestive regularity.

Barley: Contains beta-glucan, supporting cholesterol control and heart health.

Freekeh: Packed with fiber and protein, great for maintaining fullness.

Farro: Nutritious ancient grain loaded with iron and magnesium.

Steel-cut oats: Low-glycemic index for steady blood sugar levels.

Buckwheat groats: Gluten-free and rich in antioxidants like rutin.

11. Healthy Fats

Natural fats in small portions qualify as zero points due to their essential fatty acids, which promote heart health and provide satiety.

Avocado (¼ or ½): Packed with monounsaturated fats, potassium, and fiber.

Olives (fresh, unsalted): A rich source of healthy fats and antioxidants.

12. Spices, Condiments, and Miscellaneous

Low-calorie flavor enhancers elevate meals without adding points, encouraging more creative and satisfying dishes.

Spices: Cinnamon, cumin, turmeric, paprika, chili powder (anti-inflammatory properties and vibrant flavors).

Fresh Herbs: Basil, thyme, rosemary, mint (rich in antioxidants and aromatic compounds).

Condiments: Mustard, hot sauce, tamari (low sodium), vinegar (balsamic, apple cider, red wine).

Broths: Reduced-sodium chicken, vegetable, or beef stock (hydrating and adds depth to soups and stews).

Lemon and Lime: Juice and zest (brightens dishes with no calories).

Salsa (fresh, no added sugar): Tangy and loaded with vegetables.

Tomato paste (unsweetened): Concentrated source of umami.

Unsweetened cocoa powder (used sparingly): Adds richness to desserts and beverages.

13. Snacks and Small Bites

Natural, minimally processed snacks help maintain energy levels between meals while being completely guilt-free.

Air-popped popcorn (unsalted, unbuttered): Whole grain with fiber for digestive health.

Roasted chickpeas (oil-free): Crunchy and protein-packed.

Baked kale chips (homemade, no oil): A nutrient-rich alternative to crisps.

14. Beverages

Hydration is essential for metabolism, digestion, and overall health. These beverages fit seamlessly into the zero point lifestyle.

Water (plain or fruit-infused): Keeps the body hydrated and supports metabolic processes.

Unsweetened herbal teas: Soothing and naturally low in calories.

Black coffee (no sugar or cream): Boosts focus and energy without adding points.

Unsweetened almond milk: A low-calorie base for smoothies and hot beverages.

Each category of zero point foods is strategically chosen for its nutrient density, ability to keep you satiated, and low calorie-per-serving ratio. These ingredients encourage portion control naturally, making healthy eating more enjoyable and sustainable.

Seasonal Eating Guide

Seasonal eating aligns with nature's cycles, offering fresher, more nutritious foods that often qualify as zero point. Here's a seasonal breakdown to enhance your journey.

Spring

Spring is the season for detoxification and rejuvenation. Focus on zero point foods like asparagus, artichokes, radishes, and peas. Incorporate fruits such as strawberries and apricots. A sample dish is Spring Asparagus Salad with Lemon Vinaigrette.

Summer

Hydration and light eating take center stage in summer. Opt for zucchini, cucumbers, bell peppers, and watermelons. Enjoy Grilled Zucchini and Peach Salad for a refreshing meal.

Autumn

Autumn calls for heartier meals with warming ingredients. Sweet potatoes, pumpkin, and Brussels sprouts are ideal. Roasted Pumpkin Soup with Cinnamon is a perfect seasonal dish.

Winter

In winter, focus on comfort and immunity-boosting foods. Kale, cauliflower, and citrus fruits like oranges are great choices. Try a Citrus Kale Salad with Pomegranate Seeds.

Benefits of Seasonal Eating:

Better Nutrition: Seasonal foods are fresher, richer in vitamins, and more flavorful.

Cost-Effective: In-season produce is often more affordable.

Environmental Impact: Local seasonal eating reduces the carbon footprint of food transport.

These practices help you align your Zero Point Weight Loss plan with mindful choices and nature's bounty, supporting sustainable weight loss and well-being year-round.

Zero Point Dessert Recipes

Who says you can't indulge in dessert while staying on track? These zero point dessert ideas are simple, delicious, and perfect for satisfying your sweet cravings without compromising your goals.

Cinnamon-Baked Apple

Ingredients:
1 medium apple, cored and sliced
½ teaspoon ground cinnamon

Directions: 1. Preheat oven to 375°F (190°C). 2. Arrange apple slices on a baking sheet lined with parchment paper. 3. Sprinkle cinnamon over the apples and bake for 15–20 minutes until tender.

Yogurt Berry Parfait

Ingredients:
½ cup plain nonfat Greek yogurt
½ cup mixed fresh or frozen berries
1 teaspoon unsweetened cocoa powder (optional)

Directions: 1. Layer yogurt and berries in a glass. 2. Top with cocoa powder for a hint of chocolate.

Frozen Banana Bites

Ingredients:
1 medium banana, sliced into ½-inch pieces

Directions: 1. Place banana slices on a baking sheet lined with parchment paper. 2. Freeze for 1–2 hours. Serve as a cool, creamy snack. (Optional: Sprinkle with cinnamon or unsweetened cocoa powder.)

Mango Lime Sorbet

Ingredients:
1 cup frozen mango chunks
Juice of 1 lime
Directions: 1. Blend frozen mango and lime juice in a food processor until smooth. 2. Serve immediately or freeze for 10 minutes for a firmer texture.

Grilled Pineapple Rings

Ingredients:

2 pineapple rings

½ teaspoon ground cinnamon

Directions: 1. Preheat a grill or grill pan to medium heat. 2. Sprinkle cinnamon on both sides of the pineapple rings and grill for 3–4 minutes per side.

Watermelon Mint Granita

Ingredients:

2 cups diced watermelon

2 tablespoons fresh mint leaves

Directions: 1. Blend watermelon and mint in a blender until smooth. 2. Pour the mixture into a shallow dish and freeze. Scrape with a fork every 30 minutes until granita forms.

Spiced Pear Compote

Ingredients:

1 ripe pear, diced

½ teaspoon ground cinnamon

¼ teaspoon ground ginger

Directions: 1. In a small saucepan, cook the pear, cinnamon, and ginger over low heat for 10 minutes, stirring occasionally. 2. Serve warm or chilled.

Chocolate-Covered Strawberries

Ingredients:

4 large strawberries

1 teaspoon unsweetened cocoa powder

Directions: 1. Sprinkle strawberries lightly with cocoa powder. 2. Enjoy as a guilt-free chocolate-inspired treat.

Baked Cinnamon Peaches

Ingredients:

1 ripe peach, halved and pitted

½ teaspoon ground cinnamon

1 teaspoon vanilla extract

Directions: 1. Preheat the oven to 375°F (190°C). 2. Place peach halves cut side up in a baking dish. 3. Drizzle with vanilla extract and sprinkle with cinnamon. 4. Bake for 20 minutes or until the peach is tender and fragrant. 5. Serve warm as a naturally sweet and comforting dessert.

Citrus Chia Pudding

Ingredients:

1 cup unsweetened almond milk

2 tablespoons chia seeds

1 teaspoon orange zest

1 teaspoon vanilla extract

Directions: 1. In a mason jar or bowl, whisk together almond milk, chia seeds, orange zest, and vanilla extract. 2. Let sit for 5 minutes, then whisk again to prevent clumping. 3. Cover and refrigerate for at least 4 hours or overnight. 4. Serve chilled, garnished with a sprinkle of orange zest if desired.

These zero point desserts prove you don't need sugar or heavy ingredients to create delicious and satisfying treats. They are quick, easy, and perfect for any occasion!

Zero Point Salad Dressing Recipes

Elevate your salads with these flavorful, zero point dressings. Each recipe is simple, nutritious, and perfect for adding zest without adding points.

Classic Lemon Vinaigrette

Ingredients:

Juice of 1 lemon

1 teaspoon Dijon mustard

1 teaspoon minced garlic

¼ teaspoon salt

¼ teaspoon black pepper

Directions: 1. In a small bowl, whisk together lemon juice, mustard, and garlic. 2. Season with salt and pepper to taste. 3. Drizzle over salads and toss to coat.

Balsamic Herb Dressing

Ingredients:

2 tablespoons balsamic vinegar

1 teaspoon Italian seasoning (or fresh basil and oregano)

½ teaspoon garlic powder

¼ teaspoon black pepper

Directions: 1. Combine all ingredients in a jar and shake well. 2. Adjust seasoning as needed. Serve over leafy greens or roasted vegetables.

Zesty Citrus Dressing

Ingredients:

Juice of 1 orange or 2 clementines

Zest of 1 orange

1 teaspoon white vinegar

½ teaspoon grated ginger

Pinch of cayenne pepper (optional)

Directions: 1. Mix all ingredients in a small bowl until well blended. 2. Pour over salads or grilled vegetables for a tangy twist.

Spicy Mustard Dressing

Ingredients:
1 tablespoon Dijon mustard
1 tablespoon white wine vinegar
½ teaspoon paprika
¼ teaspoon ground cumin
Pinch of chili flakes (optional)

Directions: 1. Whisk all ingredients together in a small bowl. 2. Use as a dressing or dip for raw vegetables.

Creamy Yogurt Dressing

Ingredients:
½ cup plain nonfat Greek yogurt
1 tablespoon apple cider vinegar
1 teaspoon garlic powder
1 teaspoon dill or parsley, chopped
Salt and pepper to taste
Directions: 1. Stir together yogurt, vinegar, garlic powder, and herbs until smooth. 2. Add salt and pepper as needed. Ideal for coleslaw or as a ranch substitute.

Fresh Herb Dressing

Ingredients:
2 tablespoons fresh parsley, chopped
2 tablespoons fresh cilantro, chopped
1 teaspoon fresh mint, chopped
Juice of ½ lime
1 teaspoon tamari or low-sodium soy sauce

Directions: 1. Blend all ingredients in a food processor until smooth. 2. Drizzle over salads for a vibrant, herbaceous kick.

Salsa Lime Dressing

Ingredients:
3 tablespoons fresh salsa (unsweetened)
Juice of 1 lime
½ teaspoon cumin
Pinch of salt

Directions: 1. Mix all ingredients in a small bowl. 2. Use over taco salads or grain bowls for a Southwestern flair.

Vinegar and Spice Dressing

Ingredients:
2 tablespoons red wine vinegar
1 teaspoon garlic powder
1 teaspoon onion powder
¼ teaspoon smoked paprika

Directions: 1. Combine all ingredients in a bowl. 2. Stir or shake until fully blended, and drizzle over your salad.

Ginger Sesame Dressing

Ingredients:
1 teaspoon grated fresh ginger
1 teaspoon toasted sesame seeds
2 tablespoons rice vinegar
½ teaspoon tamari or soy sauce

Directions: 1. Whisk all ingredients in a small bowl. 2. Use on Asian-inspired salads or as a dipping sauce.

Simple Cucumber Mint Dressing

Ingredients:
½ cucumber, finely grated
1 tablespoon fresh mint, chopped
Juice of ½ lemon
Pinch of salt

Directions: 1. Mix all ingredients in a bowl. 2. Serve over a fresh salad or as a refreshing dip.

These zero point salad dressings are perfect for adding flavor and variety to your meals while keeping your weight loss plan on track. Adjust the seasoning and ingredients to suit your taste preferences, and enjoy guilt-free dressings for every occasion!

These bonuses are straightforward, beginner-friendly, and require minimal effort to implement, making them ideal for users just starting their zero point journey.

4-Week Meal Plan

Week 1

Day 1:
Breakfast: Herbed Tofu Scramble with Bell Pepper and Shallot
Lunch: Baked Sweet Potato and Chickpeas
Snack: Chili Lime Popcorn
Dinner: Mustard Roasted Chicken with Steamed Vegetables

Day 2:
Breakfast: Sweet Potato Breakfast Hash with Eggs
Lunch: White Bean and Kale Soup
Snack: Lemony Roasted Asparagus
Dinner: Meatballs in Creamy Almond Sauce

Day 3:
Breakfast: Orange, Banana, and Carrot Smoothie
Lunch: Mediterranean Quinoa & Garbanzo Salad
Snack: Healthy Corn, Avocado, and Tomato Medley
Dinner: Garlicky Shrimp Stir-Fry with Mushrooms

Day 4:
Breakfast: Greek Eggs and Potatoes
Lunch: French Green Lentils with Swiss Chard
Snack: Sautéed Zucchini Ribbons with Cherry Tomatoes
Dinner: Chicken Piccata with Mushrooms and Zoodles

Day 5:
Breakfast: Cauliflower Breakfast Porridge
Lunch: Turkish Eggplant and Zucchini
Snack: Citrus Marinated Olives
Dinner: Flank Steak with Citrusy Herb Pistou

Day 6:
Breakfast: Tomato Avocado Toast
Lunch: Healthy Cauliflower Rice
Snack: Salmon Stuffed Cucumbers
Dinner: Thyme Salmon with Orange and Fennel

Day 7:
Breakfast: Baked Spinach and Mushroom Egg Cups
Lunch: Garlicky Broccoli Rabe with Artichokes
Snack: Crunchy Orange Chickpeas
Dinner: Hearty Slow Cooker Quinoa Beef Stew

Week 2

Day 1:
Breakfast: Kale Stir-Fry and Fried Eggs
Lunch: Braised Greens with Olives and Walnuts
Snack: Spicy Garlic Shrimp
Dinner: Chicken with Spiced Freekeh and Preserved Lemon

Day 2:
Breakfast: Greens Smoothie with Apple and Banana
Lunch: Spinach and Brown Rice Soup
Snack: Creamy Hummus
Dinner: Braised Lamb Shanks with Bell Pepper and Harissa

Day 3:
Breakfast: Spiced Scrambled Eggs with Veggies
Lunch: Lemon Pepper Tuna Arugula Salad
Snack: Smoky Baba Ghanoush
Dinner: Roasted Branzino with Lemon and Herbs

Day 4:
Breakfast: Marinara Eggs with Parsley
Lunch: Mediterranean Veggie and Bulgur Bowl
Snack: Zesty Artichoke Antipasto
Dinner: Turkey and Butternut Squash Ragout

Day 5:
Breakfast: Shakshuka
Lunch: Mediterranean Cauliflower Rice Tabbouleh
Snack: Garlic Butter Sautéed Mushrooms
Dinner: Simple Pork Souvlaki

Day 6:
Breakfast: Spanish Tuna Tortilla with Potatoes
Lunch: Ratatouille with Pesto
Snack: Spicy Roasted Red Potatoes
Dinner: Baked Grouper with Tomatoes and Olives

Day 7:
Breakfast: Sweet Potato Hash with Mushrooms
Lunch: Moroccan Vegetable Tagine
Snack: Mediterranean Trail Mix
Dinner: Lemon Rosemary Lamb Chops

Week 3

Day 1:
Breakfast: Sweet Potato Breakfast Hash with Eggs
Lunch: Spanish Green Beans with Tomatoes
Snack: Baked Kale Chips
Dinner: Grilled Chicken Kebabs with Zucchini and Olives

Day 2:
Breakfast: Minty Spinach Avocado Smoothie
Lunch: Mediterranean Style Egg Salad
Snack: Air Fryer Sea Salt Beet Chips
Dinner: Lamb Shanks Stew with Carrots

Day 3:
Breakfast: Herbed Tofu Scramble with Bell Pepper and Shallot
Lunch: Simple Tomato Basil Soup
Snack: Chili Lime Popcorn
Dinner: Swordfish in Citrusy Tarragon Butter

Day 4:
Breakfast: Greek Eggs and Potatoes
Lunch: Lemony Avocado Farro Bowl
Snack: Lemony Roasted Asparagus
Dinner: Roasted Chicken with Cauliflower and Tomatoes

Day 5:
Breakfast: Kale Stir-Fry and Fried Eggs
Lunch: Braised Radishes with Peas and Mushrooms
Snack: Healthy Corn, Avocado, and Tomato Medley
Dinner: Spanish Pepper Steak with Onions

Day 6:
Breakfast: Orange, Banana, and Carrot Smoothie
Lunch: Cauliflower and Carrot Hash
Snack: Sautéed Zucchini Ribbons with Cherry Tomatoes
Dinner: Fried Fishcakes with Zucchini Salad

Day 7:
Breakfast: Tomato Avocado Toast
Lunch: Oven Roasted Acorn Squash
Snack: Citrus Marinated Olives
Dinner: Homemade Beef Sliders with Pepper Slaw

Week 4

Day 1:
Breakfast: Cauliflower Breakfast Porridge
Lunch: Sautéed Garlic Spinach with Lemon
Snack: Salmon Stuffed Cucumbers
Dinner: Bake Lemon Chicken Thighs Foil Packets

Day 2:
Breakfast: Spiced Scrambled Eggs with Veggies
Lunch: Gigante Bean Soup with Celery and Olives
Snack: Crunchy Orange Chickpeas
Dinner: Air Fryer Lamb Kofta with Mint-Yogurt Sauce

Day 3:
Breakfast: Greens Smoothie with Apple and Banana
Lunch: Bulgur Salad with Carrots and Almonds
Snack: Spicy Garlic Shrimp
Dinner: Italian Beef Short Rib Stew

Day 4:
Breakfast: Marinara Eggs with Parsley
Lunch: Lentils and Bulgur with Caramelized Onions
Snack: Creamy Hummus
Dinner: Whole Roast Chicken with Potatoes

Day 5:
Breakfast: Shakshuka
Lunch: Spiced Cauliflower Couscous
Snack: Smoky Baba Ghanoush
Dinner: Grilled Beef Kefta

Day 6:
Breakfast: Baked Spinach and Mushroom Egg Cups
Lunch: Sautéed Zucchini with Garlic and Mint
Snack: Zesty Artichoke Antipasto
Dinner: Cilantro-Lemon Shrimp

Day 7:
Breakfast: Sweet Potato Hash with Mushrooms
Lunch: Sugar Snap Pea and Barley Salad
Snack: Garlic Butter Sautéed Mushrooms
Dinner: Seared Scallops with Vegetables

Chapter 1 Breakfast Recipes

Sweet Potato Breakfast Hash with Eggs

Prep Time: 10 minutes | Cook Time: 20 minutes | Serves: 4

2 tablespoons extra-virgin olive oil

3 cups peeled and cubed sweet potato (½-inch pieces) (2 to 3 sweet potatoes)

1 cup diced yellow bell pepper

1 cup diced yellow onion

1 teaspoon paprika

¼ teaspoon salt

3 cups chopped kale

2 garlic cloves, minced

4 pasteurized large eggs

⅛ teaspoon freshly ground black pepper

Salsa, for serving (optional)

1. In a large skillet, heat the olive oil over medium-high heat. Add the sweet potato, onion, bell pepper, paprika, and salt. Cook for around 10 minutes, stirring frequently, or until the potatoes start to soften. 2. Add the kale and garlic, stirring to combine. Cook until the kale begins to wilt, about 3 minutes. 3. Reduce the heat to low. With a spoon or spatula, create 4 pockets for the eggs in the sweet potato mixture. Crack 1 egg into each pocket. Cover the skillet and cook until the egg whites are set and the yolk is slightly runny, about 5 minutes. 4. Remove from the heat and season with the pepper. Serve as is, or with your favorite salsa, if desired. Store any leftovers in an airtight container in the refrigerator for up to 5 days.
Per Serving: Calories 181; Fat 11.97g; Sodium 226mg; Carbs 11.25g; Fiber 3.2g; Sugar 2.23g; Protein 8.54g

Greek Eggs and Potatoes

Prep Time: 5 minutes | Cook Time: 30 minutes | Serves: 4

3 medium tomatoes, seeded and coarsely chopped

2 tablespoons fresh chopped basil

1 garlic clove, minced

2 tablespoons plus ½ cup olive oil, divided

Sea salt and freshly ground pepper, to taste

3 large russet potatoes

4 large eggs

1 teaspoon fresh oregano, chopped

1. Put tomatoes in a food processor and puree them, skins and all. 2. Add the basil, sea salt, garlic, 2 tablespoons olive oil, and freshly ground pepper, and pulse to combine. 3. Put the mixture in a large skillet over low heat and cook, covered, for 20–25 minutes, or until the sauce has thickened and is bubbly. 4. Meanwhile, dice the potatoes into small cubes. Put ½ cup olive oil in a nonstick skillet over medium-low heat. 5. Fry the potatoes for 5 minutes until crisp and browned on the outside, then cover and reduce heat to low. Steam the potatoes until done. 6. Gently crack the eggs into the tomato sauce. Cook over low heat until the eggs are set in the sauce, about 6 minutes. 7. Remove the potatoes from the pan and drain them on paper towels, then place them in a bowl. 8. Sprinkle with the freshly ground pepper and sea salt to taste and top with the oregano. 9. Carefully remove the eggs with a slotted spoon and place them on a plate with the potatoes. Spoon the sauce over the top and serve.
Per Serving: Calories 369; Fat 11.94g; Sodium 381mg; Carbs 54.6g; Fiber 4.9g; Sugar 4.35g; Protein 13.16g

Herbed Tofu Scramble with Bell Pepper and Shallot

Prep Time: 10 minutes | Cook Time: 7 minutes | Serves: 4

14 ounces soft tofu, drained and patted dry

1½ teaspoons canola oil

1 small red bell pepper, stemmed, seeded, and chopped fine

1 shallot, minced

½ teaspoon salt

¼ teaspoon ground curry powder

⅛ teaspoon pepper

2 tablespoons minced fresh basil, parsley, tarragon, or marjoram

1. Crumble the tofu into ¼- to ½-inch pieces. Spread the tofu on paper towel–lined baking sheet and allow to drain for 20 minutes, then gently press dry with additional paper towels. Heat the oil in 10-inch nonstick skillet over medium heat until shimmering. Add the bell pepper and shallot and cook until softened, about 5 minutes. 2. Stir the in tofu, salt, curry powder, and pepper and cook until tofu is heated through, about 2 minutes. Off heat, stir in the basil. Serve.

Per Serving: Calories 84; Fat 5.45g; Sodium 300mg; Carbs 3.57g; Fiber 0.8g; Sugar 1.75g; Protein 6.83g

Kale Stir-Fry and Fried Eggs

Prep Time: 10 minutes | Cook Time: 15 minutes | Serves: 4

2 tablespoons extra virgin olive oil

1 onion, finely chopped

1 red pepper, finely sliced

2 garlic cloves, finely sliced

A little finely chopped hot red or green chilli or a pinch of chilli flakes

10 cherry tomatoes, halved or quartered

400g (14oz) kale, Cavolo Nero or other cabbage, shredded

2 tablespoons ghee, lard or dripping

4 eggs

Salt and freshly ground black pepper

1. Heat the oil in a large frying pan. Add the onion, red pepper, garlic, chilli (to taste) and some seasoning and fry over a medium heat for about 5 minutes, then add the tomatoes and cook for 2 minutes or until softened. 2. Meanwhile, boil or steam the kale for about 5 minutes until soft. Drain and add to the pan. Toss through, then taste and season as necessary. 3. To fry the eggs, add the fat to a frying pan over a medium-high heat. When it feels hot to your hand held above it, crack the eggs into the pan, socially distanced apart if your pan allows it. Season the eggs with a little salt and pepper. Fry for a couple of minutes or until you can see the white is mainly opaque and the yolk is starting to set. Remove them from the pan if you like them runny. If not, leave for longer or flip over with a spatula and leave for 30 seconds. This will give you eggs over easy, meaning the whites are cooked through and just the centers of the yolks are runny – just how I like them. 4. Serve the kale stir-fry in warm bowls topped with the fried eggs.

Per Serving: Calories 260; Fat 18.47g; Sodium 397mg; Carbs 16.03g; Fiber 5g; Sugar 5.89g; Protein 11.04g

Greens Smoothie with Apple and Banana

Prep Time: 5 minutes | Cook Time: 0 minute | Serves: 2

1 cup 1% low-fat milk

1 cup plain nonfat Greek yogurt

2 cups packed leafy greens (spinach, kale, or spring greens)

¼ medium avocado

1 medium Granny Smith apple, cored and sliced

1 medium banana, sliced and frozen

1. Put the milk, yogurt, avocado, leafy greens, apple, and banana into a high-powered blender. Blend for 30 to 60 seconds or until smooth. 2. Pour into two glasses. Serve immediately.

Per Serving: Calories 227; Fat 4.61g; Sodium 113mg; Carbs 36.22g; Fiber 6.2g; Sugar 23.45g; Protein 12.68g

Orange, Banana, and Carrot Smoothie

Prep Time: 10 minutes | Cook Time: 0 minute | Serves: 2

1 cup 1% low-fat milk

½ cup plain nonfat Greek yogurt

1 medium orange, peeled and sectioned

1 medium banana, sliced and frozen

1 medium carrot, coarsely chopped

1 teaspoon vanilla extract

2 teaspoons grated orange zest

1. Put the milk, yogurt, orange, carrot, banana, vanilla, and orange zest into a high-powered blender. Blend for 30 to 60 seconds or until smooth. 2. Pour into two glasses. Serve immediately.

Per Serving: Calories 194; Fat 1.8g; Sodium 98mg; Carbs 34.19g; Fiber 4.1g; Sugar 23.17g; Protein 11.82g

Minty Spinach Avocado Smoothie

Prep Time: 5 minutes | Cook Time: 0 minute | Serves: 1

1 small very ripe avocado, peeled and pitted

1 cup almond milk or water, plus more as needed

1 cup tender baby spinach leaves, stems removed

½ medium cucumber, peeled and seeded

1 tablespoon extra-virgin olive oil or avocado oil

8 to 10 fresh mint leaves, stems removed

Juice of 1 lime (about 1 to 2 tablespoons)

1. In a blender or a large wide-mouth jar, if using an immersion blender, combine the avocado, almond milk, spinach, cucumber, olive oil, lime juice, and mint and blend until smooth and creamy, adding more almond milk or water to achieve your desired consistency.

Per Serving: Calories 471; Fat 43.28g; Sodium 46mg; Carbs 24.11g; Fiber 15g; Sugar 3.58g; Protein 5.66g

Spanish Tuna Tortilla with Potatoes

Prep Time: 15 minutes | Cook Time: 15 minutes | Serves: 4

6 large eggs

¼ cup olive oil

2 small russet potatoes, diced

1 small onion, chopped

1 roasted red bell pepper, sliced

1 (7-ounce) can tuna packed in water, drained well and flaked

2 plum tomatoes, seeded and diced

1 teaspoon dried tarragon

1. Preheat the broiler on high. 2. In a large bowl, crack the eggs and whisk until just combined. Heat the olive oil in a large, oven-safe, nonstick or cast-iron skillet over medium-low heat. 3. Add the potatoes and cook for about 7 minutes, until slightly soft. Add the onion and the peppers and cook until soft, 3–5 minutes. 4. Add the tuna, tomatoes, and tarragon, stirring to combine, then add the eggs. 5. Cook for 7–10 minutes until the eggs are bubbling from the bottom and the bottom is slightly brown. 6. Place the skillet into the oven on 1 of the first 2 racks, and cook until the middle is set and the top is slightly brown. 7. Slice into wedges and serve warm or at room temperature.

Per Serving: Calories 369; Fat 21.23g; Sodium 182mg; Carbs 19.93g; Fiber 2g; Sugar 3.16g; Protein 24.57g

Cauliflower Breakfast Porridge

Prep Time: 5 minutes | Cook Time: 5 minutes | Serves: 2

2 cups riced cauliflower

¾ cup unsweetened almond, flax, or hemp milk

4 tablespoons extra-virgin olive oil, divided

2 teaspoons grated fresh orange peel (from ½ orange)

½ teaspoon ground cinnamon

½ teaspoon almond extract or vanilla extract

⅛ teaspoon salt

4 tablespoons chopped walnuts, divided

1. In medium saucepan, combine the riced cauliflower, almond milk, 2 tablespoons olive oil, grated orange peel, almond extract, cinnamon, and salt. Stir to combine and bring just to a boil over medium-high heat, stirring constantly. 2. Remove from heat and stir in 2 tablespoons chopped walnuts. Stir to combine. 3. Divide into bowls, topping each with 1 tablespoon of chopped walnuts and 1 tablespoon of the remaining olive oil.

Per Serving: Calories 414; Fat 36.88g; Sodium 252mg; Carbs 15.12g; Fiber 4.8g; Sugar 7.88g; Protein 10.04g

Shakshuka

Prep Time: 5 minutes | Cook Time: 20 minutes | Serves: 4

2 tablespoons extra-virgin olive oil

1 cup chopped shallots

1 cup chopped red bell peppers

1 cup finely diced potato

1 teaspoon garlic powder

1 (14.5-ounce) can diced tomatoes, drained

¼ teaspoon turmeric

¼ teaspoon paprika

¼ teaspoon ground cardamom

4 large eggs

¼ cup chopped fresh cilantro

1. Preheat the oven to 350°F. 2. In an oven-safe sauté pan or skillet, heat the olive oil over medium-high heat and sauté the shallots, stirring occasionally, for about 3 minutes, until fragrant. Add the bell peppers, potato, and garlic powder. Cook, uncovered, for 10 minutes, stirring every 2 minutes. 3. Add the tomatoes, paprika, turmeric, and cardamom to the skillet and mix well. Once bubbly, remove from heat and crack the eggs into the skillet so the yolks are facing up. 4. Put the skillet in the oven and cook for an additional 5 to 10 minutes, until eggs are cooked to your preference. Garnish with the cilantro and serve.

Per Serving: Calories 200; Fat 11.93g; Sodium 196mg; Carbs 15.67g; Fiber 4.1g; Sugar 5.49g; Protein 8.72g

Tomato Avocado Toast

Prep Time: 5 minutes | Cook Time: 5 minutes | Serves: 2

2 tablespoons ground flaxseed

½ teaspoon baking powder

2 large eggs

1 teaspoon salt, plus more for serving

½ teaspoon freshly ground black pepper, plus more for serving

½ teaspoon garlic powder, sesame seed, caraway seed or other dried herbs (optional)

3 tablespoons extra-virgin olive oil, divided

1 medium ripe avocado, peeled, pitted, and sliced

2 tablespoons chopped ripe tomato or salsa

1. In a small bowl, combine the flaxseed and baking powder, breaking up any lumps in the baking powder. Add the eggs, pepper, salt, and garlic powder (if using) and whisk well. Let sit for 2 minutes. 2. In a small nonstick skillet, heat 1 tablespoon olive oil over medium heat. Pour the egg mixture into the skillet and let cook undisturbed until the egg begins to set on bottom, 2 to 3 minutes. 3. Using a rubber spatula, scrape down the sides to allow uncooked egg to reach the bottom. Cook for another 2 to 3 minutes. 4. Once almost set, flip like a pancake and allow the top to fully cook, another 1 to 2 minutes. 5. Remove from the pan and allow to cool slightly. Slice into 2 pieces. 6. Top each "toast" with avocado slices, additional salt and pepper, chopped tomato, and drizzle with the remaining 2 tablespoons olive oil.

Per Serving: Calories 412; Fat 38.5g; Sodium 1370mg; Carbs 11.02g; Fiber 7.1g; Sugar 1.23g; Protein 9.37g

Spiced Scrambled Eggs with Veggies

Prep Time: 15 minutes | Cook Time: 28 minutes | Serves: 4

2 tablespoons olive oil

1 small red onion, chopped

1 medium green pepper, cored, seeded, and finely chopped

1 red Fresno or jalapeño chili pepper, seeded and cut into thin strips

3 medium tomatoes, chopped

Sea salt and freshly ground pepper, to taste

1 tablespoon ground cumin

1 teaspoon ground coriander

4 large eggs, lightly beaten

1. Heat the olive oil in a large, heavy skillet over medium heat. 2. Add the onion and cook until soft and translucent, 6–7 minutes. 3. Stir in the peppers and cook for an additional 4–5 minutes, until tender. Add the tomatoes and season to taste. 4. Stir in the cumin and coriander. 5. Simmer for 10 minutes over medium-low heat. 6. Add the eggs, gently stirring them into the mixture to distribute. 7. Cover the skillet and cook until the eggs are set but still fluffy and tender, about 5–6 minutes more. 8. Divide between 4 plates and serve immediately.

Per Serving: Calories 170; Fat 12.12g; Sodium 372mg; Carbs 8.5g; Fiber 2g; Sugar 4.56g; Protein 8.02g

Marinara Eggs with Parsley

Prep Time: 5 minutes | Cook Time: 15 minutes | Serves: 6

1 tablespoon extra-virgin olive oil

1 cup chopped onion (about ½ medium onion)

2 garlic cloves, minced (about 1 teaspoon)

2 (14.5-ounce) cans Italian diced tomatoes, undrained, no salt

added

6 large eggs

½ cup chopped fresh flat-leaf (Italian) parsley

1. In a large skillet over medium-high heat, heat the oil. Add the onion and cook for 5 minutes, stirring occasionally. Add the garlic and cook for 1 minute. 2. Pour the tomatoes with their juices over the onion mixture and cook until bubbling, 2 to 3 minutes. While waiting for the tomato mixture to bubble, crack one egg into a small custard cup or coffee mug. 3. When the tomato mixture bubbles, lower the heat to medium. Then use a large spoon to make six indentations in the tomato mixture. Gently pour the first cracked egg into one indentation and repeat, cracking the remaining eggs, one at a time, into the custard cup and pouring one into each indentation. Cover the skillet and cook for 6 to 7 minutes, or until the eggs are done to your liking (about 6 minutes for soft-cooked, 7 minutes for harder cooked). 4. Top with the parsley and serve.

Per Serving: Calories 133; Fat 7.98g; Sodium 97mg; Carbs 7.6g; Fiber 3.1g; Sugar 4.57g; Protein 8.54g

Baked Spinach and Mushroom Egg Cups

Prep Time: 5 minutes | Cook Time: 15 minutes | Serves: 6

Olive oil cooking spray
6 large eggs
1 garlic clove, minced
½ teaspoon salt
½ teaspoon black pepper

Pinch red pepper flakes
8 ounces baby bella mushrooms, sliced
1 cup fresh baby spinach
2 scallions, white parts and green parts, diced

1. Preheat the air fryer to 320°F. Lightly coat the inside of six silicone muffin cups or a six-cup muffin tin with olive oil cooking spray. 2. In a large bowl, beat the eggs, garlic, pepper, salt, and red pepper flakes for 1 to 2 minutes, or until well combined. 3. Fold in the mushrooms, spinach, and scallions. 4. Divide the mixture evenly among the muffin cups. 5. Place into the air fryer and bake for 12 to 15 minutes, or until the eggs are set. 6. Remove and allow to cool for 5 minutes before serving.

Per Serving: Calories 87; Fat 4.98g; Sodium 272mg; Carbs 3.19g; Fiber 0.8g; Sugar 1.46g; Protein 7.89g

Sweet Potato Hash with Mushrooms

Prep Time: 15 minutes | Cook Time: 18 minutes | Serves: 6

2 medium sweet potatoes, peeled and cut into 1-inch cubes
½ green bell pepper, diced
½ red onion, diced
4 ounces baby bella mushrooms, diced
2 tablespoons olive oil

1 garlic clove, minced
½ teaspoon salt
½ teaspoon black pepper
½ tablespoon chopped fresh rosemary

1. Preheat the air fryer to 380°F. 2. In a large bowl, toss all ingredients together until the vegetables are well coated and seasonings distributed. 3. Pour the vegetables into the air fryer basket, making sure they are in a single even layer. (If using a smaller air fryer, you may need to do this in two batches.) 4. Roast for 9 minutes, then toss or flip the vegetables. Roast for 9 minutes more. 5. Transfer to a serving bowl or individual plates and enjoy.

Per Serving: Calories 85; Fat 4.66g; Sodium 209mg; Carbs 10.05g; Fiber 1.7g; Sugar 3.42g; Protein 1.59g

Chapter 2 Vegetable and Side Recipes

Baked Sweet Potato and Chickpeas

Prep Time: 10 minutes | Cook Time: 25 minutes | Serves: 4

1 large sweet potato, peeled and cut into ½-inch pieces

2 (15-ounce) cans chickpeas, drained, rinsed, and patted dry

1 medium zucchini, sliced

1 medium red bell pepper, seeded and sliced

½ yellow onion, sliced

2 garlic cloves, minced

2 tablespoons extra-virgin olive oil

1 teaspoon paprika

1 teaspoon Italian seasoning

½ teaspoon salt

¼ teaspoon freshly ground black pepper

1. Preheat the oven to 425°F. Line a baking sheet with a silicone baking mat or parchment paper. 2. In a large bowl, toss together the sweet potato, bell pepper, onion, chickpeas, zucchini, garlic, olive oil, paprika, salt, Italian seasoning, and pepper. Arrange the mixture on the prepared baking sheet in a single layer. If needed, use two baking sheets to spread them out evenly. Bake for 25 minutes, stirring halfway through, until the potatoes are tender and the vegetables have reached your desired level of crispiness. Serve hot. 3. Refrigerate the leftovers in an airtight container for up to 5 days.

Per Serving: Calories 298; Fat 10.52g; Sodium 673mg; Carbs 42.31g; Fiber 10.8g; Sugar 9.98g; Protein 10.57g

Healthy Cauliflower Rice

Prep Time: 10 minutes | Cook Time: 12-14 minutes | Serves: 4

400g (14oz) cauliflower (flower, stalk and leaves), broccoli or sprouts

2 tablespoons extra virgin olive oil, ghee, coconut oil, chicken

fat or beef dripping

1 small onion or leek, or 5 spring onions, finely chopped

Salt and freshly ground black pepper

1. Cut the head of the cauliflower into large florets and roughly chop the stalk and leaves. Put a third of the cauliflower into a food processor and pulse until finely chopped (it will resemble large grains of rice), making sure you don't end up with a purée. Tip into a bowl and repeat with the remaining two thirds. If you don't have a food processor, coarsely grate the florets and stalk and finely chop the leaves. 2. Heat the fat in a wok or large frying pan. Fry the onion over medium heat for 5–7 minutes, or until soft. Add the cauliflower rice, season and stir through. Add 75ml (2½fl oz) water, cover, and cook over a low heat for about 7 minutes or until just soft, stirring occasionally.

Per Serving: Calories 92; Fat 7.06g; Sodium 322mg; Carbs 6.8g; Fiber 2.4g; Sugar 2.65g; Protein 2.14g

Turkish Eggplant and Zucchini

Prep Time: 10 minutes | Cook Time: 15-20 minutes | Serves: 6

1 medium eggplant

1 zucchini

1 onion

1 red pepper

4 tablespoons extra virgin olive oil

2 garlic cloves, crushed

½ teaspoon chilli flakes (optional)

400g (14oz) can chopped tomatoes or 400g (14oz) passata

1 tablespoon red wine or other vinegar

6 tablespoons Greek yogurt (optional)

Salt and freshly ground black pepper

1. Cut the vegetables into bite-sized pieces. 2. Pour the oil into a large frying pan or wok over a high heat, add the vegetables, garlic and chilli, if using, season and stir-fry for 10 minutes. 3. Stir in the tomatoes and vinegar, then bring to a boil. Reduce the heat to medium and cook for a further 5–10 minutes to thicken. Taste and add further seasoning as necessary. 4. Serve with the yogurt, if using.

Per Serving: Calories 137; Fat 9.64g; Sodium 237mg; Carbs 11.54g; Fiber 3.9g; Sugar 5.54g; Protein 2.95g

Garlicky Broccoli Rabe with Artichokes

Prep Time: 5 minutes | Cook Time: 10 minutes | Serves: 4

2 pounds fresh broccoli rabe

½ cup extra-virgin olive oil, divided

3 garlic cloves, finely minced

1 teaspoon salt

1 teaspoon red pepper flakes

1 (13.75-ounce) can artichoke hearts, drained and quartered

1 tablespoon water

2 tablespoons red wine vinegar

Freshly ground black pepper

1. Trim away any thick lower stems and yellow leaves from the broccoli rabe and discard. Cut into individual florets with a couple inches of thin stem attached. 2. In a large skillet, heat ¼ cup olive oil over medium-high heat. Add the trimmed broccoli, salt, garlic, and red pepper flakes and sauté for 5 minutes, until the broccoli begins to soften. Add the artichoke hearts and sauté for another 2 minutes. 3. Add the water and reduce the heat to low. Cover and simmer until the broccoli stems are tender, 3 to 5 minutes. 4. In a small bowl, whisk together remaining ¼ cup olive oil and the vinegar. Drizzle over the broccoli and artichokes. Season with the ground black pepper, if desired.

Per Serving: Calories 346; Fat 28.47g; Sodium 716mg; Carbs 19.11g; Fiber 14.6g; Sugar 1.88g; Protein 10.19g

Braised Greens with Olives and Walnuts

Prep Time: 5 minutes | Cook Time: 20 minutes | Serves: 4

8 cups fresh greens (such as kale, mustard greens, spinach, or chard)

2 to 4 garlic cloves, finely minced

½ cup roughly chopped pitted green or black olives

½ cup roughly chopped shelled walnuts

¼ cup extra-virgin olive oil

2 tablespoons red wine vinegar

1 to 2 teaspoons freshly chopped herbs such as oregano, basil, rosemary, or thyme

1. Remove the tough stems from the greens and chop into bite-size pieces. Place in a large rimmed skillet or pot. 2. Turn the heat to high and add the minced garlic and enough water to just cover the greens. Bring to a boil, then reduce the heat to low and simmer until the greens are wilted and tender and most of the liquid has evaporated, adding more if the greens start to burn. For more tender greens such as spinach, this may only take 5 minutes, while tougher greens such as chard may need up to 20 minutes. When finished, remove from the heat and add the chopped olives and walnuts. 3. In a small bowl, whisk together the olive oil, vinegar, and herbs. Drizzle over the cooked greens and toss to coat. Serve warm.

Per Serving: Calories 250; Fat 23.57g; Sodium 29mg; Carbs 7.84g; Fiber 4.6g; Sugar 1.88g; Protein 5.55g

Ratatouille with Pesto

Prep Time: 15 minutes | Cook Time: 10 minutes | Serves: 4

2 tablespoons extra-virgin olive oil

2 red or yellow bell peppers, stemmed, seeded, and cut into 1-inch pieces

1 onion, chopped fine

1 teaspoon table salt

4 garlic cloves, minced

1 teaspoon herbes de Provence

¼ teaspoon red pepper flakes

1 (28-ounce) can whole peeled tomatoes, drained with juice reserved, chopped

1 pound eggplant, cut into ½-inch pieces

1 pound zucchini, quartered lengthwise and sliced 1 inch thick

1 tablespoon sherry vinegar

¼ cup basil pesto, plus extra for serving

1. Using the highest sauté function, heat the oil in the instant pot until shimmering. Add the bell peppers, onion, and salt and cook for about 5 minutes, until the vegetables are softened. Stir in the garlic, herbes de Provence, and pepper flakes and cook until fragrant, about 30 seconds. Stir in the tomatoes and reserved juice, eggplant, and zucchini. Lock the lid in place and close the pressure release valve. Set to the high pressure cook function and cook for 1 minute. 2. Turn off the instant pot and quickly release pressure. Carefully remove the lid, ensuring the steam escapes away from you. Using the highest sauté function, continue to cook the vegetable mixture until the zucchini is tender and sauce has thickened slightly, 3 to 5 minutes. Stir in the vinegar and season with the salt and pepper to taste. Dollop individual portions with the pesto and serve, passing extra pesto separately.

Per Serving: Calories 262, Fat 16.63g, Sodium 939mg, Carbs 24.97g, Fiber 10.4g, Sugar 12.92g, Protein 8.37g

Moroccan Vegetable Tagine

Prep Time: 20 minutes | Cook Time: 1 hour | Serves: 6

½ cup extra-virgin olive oil

2 medium yellow onions, sliced

6 celery stalks, sliced into ¼-inch crescents

6 garlic cloves, minced

1 teaspoon ground cumin

1 teaspoon ginger powder

1 teaspoon salt

½ teaspoon paprika

½ teaspoon ground cinnamon

¼ teaspoon freshly ground black pepper

2 cups vegetable stock

1 medium eggplant, cut into 1-inch cubes

2 medium zucchini, cut into ½-inch-thick semicircles

2 cups cauliflower florets

1 (13.75-ounce) can artichoke hearts, drained and quartered

1 cup halved and pitted green olives

½ cup chopped fresh flat-leaf parsley, for garnish

½ cup chopped fresh cilantro leaves, for garnish

Greek yogurt, non-fat and plain, for garnish (optional)

1. In a large, thick soup pot or Dutch oven, heat the olive oil over medium-high heat. Add the onion and celery and sauté until softened, 6 to 8 minutes. Add the garlic, cumin, paprika, ginger, salt, cinnamon, and pepper and sauté for another 2 minutes. 2. Pour in the stock and bring to a boil. Reduce the heat to low and add the zucchini, eggplant, and cauliflower. Simmer on low heat, covered, until the vegetables are tender, 30 to 35 minutes. Add the artichoke hearts and olives, cover, and simmer for another 15 minutes. 3. Serve garnished with parsley, cilantro, and Greek yogurt (if using).

Per Serving: Calories 310; Fat 21.84g; Sodium 820mg; Carbs 27.37g; Fiber 12.4g; Sugar 7.66g; Protein 6.49g

Sautéed Garlic Spinach with Lemon

Prep Time: 5 minutes | Cook Time: 10 minutes | Serves: 4

¼ cup extra-virgin olive oil

1 large onion, thinly sliced

3 cloves garlic, minced

6 (1-pound) bags of baby spinach, washed

½ teaspoon salt

1 lemon, cut into wedges

1. Cook the olive oil, onion, and garlic in a large skillet for 2 minutes over medium heat. 2. Add one bag of spinach and ½ teaspoon of salt. Cover the skillet and allow the spinach to wilt for 30 seconds. Repeat (omitting the salt), adding 1 bag of spinach at a time. 3. Once all the spinach has been added, remove the cover and cook for 3 minutes, letting some of the moisture evaporate. 4. Serve warm with a generous squeeze of lemon over the top.

Per Serving: Calories 166; Fat 14.02g; Sodium 383mg; Carbs 9.19g; Fiber 3.2g; Sugar 2.39g; Protein 3.84g

Spanish Green Beans with Tomatoes

Prep Time: 10 minutes | Cook Time: 20 minutes | Serves: 4

¼ cup extra-virgin olive oil

1 large onion, chopped

4 cloves garlic, finely chopped

1 pound green beans, fresh or frozen, trimmed

1½ teaspoons salt, divided

1 (15-ounce) can diced tomatoes

½ teaspoon freshly ground black pepper

1. In a large pot over medium heat, heat the olive oil, onion, and garlic; cook for 1 minute. 2. Cut the green beans into 2-inch pieces. 3. Add the green beans and 1 teaspoon of salt to the pot and toss everything together; cook for 3 minutes. 4. Add the diced tomatoes, remaining ½ teaspoon of salt, and black pepper to the pot; continue to cook for another 12 minutes, stirring occasionally. 5. Serve warm.

Per Serving: Calories 192; Fat 14.08g; Sodium 1003mg; Carbs 16.28g; Fiber 5.9g; Sugar 8.03g; Protein 3.55g

Mediterranean Cauliflower Rice Tabbouleh

Prep Time: 15 minutes | Cook Time: 5 minutes | Serves: 6

6 tablespoons extra-virgin olive oil, divided

4 cups riced cauliflower

3 garlic cloves, finely minced

1½ teaspoons salt

½ teaspoon freshly ground black pepper

½ large cucumber, peeled, seeded, and chopped

½ cup chopped mint leaves

½ cup chopped Italian parsley

½ cup chopped pitted Kalamata olives

2 tablespoons minced red onion

Juice of 1 lemon (about 2 tablespoons)

2 cups baby arugula or spinach leaves

2 medium avocados, peeled, pitted, and diced

1 cup quartered cherry tomatoes

1. In a large skillet, heat 2 tablespoons of olive oil over medium-high heat. Add the riced cauliflower, salt, garlic, and pepper and sauté until just tender but not mushy, 3 to 4 minutes. Remove from the heat and place in a large bowl. 2. Add the cucumber, mint, parsley, red onion, lemon juice, olives, and remaining 4 tablespoons olive oil and toss well. Place in the refrigerator, uncovered, and refrigerate for at least 30 minutes, or up to 2 hours. 3. Before serving, add the arugula, avocado, and tomatoes and toss to combine well. Season to taste with the salt and pepper and serve cold or at room temperature.

Per Serving: Calories 275; Fat 24.95g; Sodium 698mg; Carbs 13.8g; Fiber 7.3g; Sugar 3.32g; Protein 3.74g

Cauliflower and Carrot Hash

Prep Time: 10 minutes | Cook Time: 10 minutes | Serves: 4

3 tablespoons extra-virgin olive oil

1 large onion, chopped

1 tablespoon garlic, minced

2 cups carrots, diced

4 cups cauliflower pieces, washed

1 teaspoon salt

½ teaspoon ground cumin

1. In a large skillet over medium heat, cook the olive oil, onion, garlic, and carrots for 3 minutes. 2. Cut the cauliflower into 1-inch or bite-size pieces. Add the cauliflower, salt, and cumin to the skillet and toss to combine with the carrots and onions. 3. Cover and cook for 3 minutes. 4. Toss the vegetables and continue to cook uncovered for another 3 to 4 minutes. 5. Serve warm.

Per Serving: Calories 162; Fat 10.69g; Sodium 660mg; Carbs 15.78g; Fiber 4.6g; Sugar 6.69g; Protein 3.25g

Braised Radishes with Peas and Mushrooms

Prep Time: 20 minutes | Cook Time: 5 minutes | Serves: 4

¼ cup extra-virgin olive oil, divided

1 shallot, sliced thin

3 garlic cloves, sliced thin

1½ pounds radishes, 2 cups greens reserved, radishes trimmed and halved if small or quartered if large

½ cup water

½ teaspoon table salt

8 ounces sugar snap peas, strings removed, sliced thin on bias

8 ounces cremini mushrooms, trimmed and sliced thin

2 teaspoons grated lemon zest plus 1 teaspoon juice

1 cup plain Greek yogurt

½ cup fresh cilantro leaves

3 tablespoons dukkah

1. Using the highest sauté function, heat 2 tablespoons oil in the instant pot until shimmering. Add the shallot and cook until softened, about 2 minutes. Stir in the garlic and cook until fragrant, about 30 seconds. Stir in the radishes, water, and salt. Lock the lid in place and close the pressure release valve. Set to the high pressure cook function and cook for 1 minute. 2. Turn off the instant pot and quickly release pressure. Carefully remove the lid, ensuring the steam escapes away from you. Stir in the snap peas, cover, and let sit until heated through, about 3 minutes. Add the radish greens, mushrooms, lemon zest and juice, and remaining 2 tablespoons oil and gently toss to combine. Season with the salt and pepper to taste. 3. Spread ¼ cup yogurt over bottom of 4 individual serving plates. Using a slotted spoon, arrange the vegetable mixture on top and sprinkle with the cilantro and dukkah. Serve.

Per Serving: Calories 229; Fat 16g; Sodium 362mg; Carbs 17.16g; Fiber 4.9g; Sugar 10.7g; Protein 6.71g

Oven Roasted Acorn Squash

Prep Time: 10 minutes | Cook Time: 35 minutes | Serves: 6

2 acorn squash, medium to large
2 tablespoons extra-virgin olive oil
1 teaspoon salt, plus more for seasoning
5 tablespoons unsalted butter

¼ cup chopped sage leaves
2 tablespoons fresh thyme leaves
½ teaspoon freshly ground black pepper

1. Preheat the oven to 400°F. 2. Cut the acorn squash in half lengthwise. Use a spoon to scrape out the seeds, then cut it horizontally into ¾-inch-thick slices. 3. In a large bowl, drizzle the squash with the olive oil, sprinkle with salt, and toss together to coat. 4. Lay the acorn squash flat on a baking sheet. 5. Place the baking sheet in the oven and bake the squash for 20 minutes. Flip squash over with a spatula and bake for another 15 minutes. 6. Melt the butter in a medium saucepan over medium heat. 7. Add the sage and thyme to the melted butter and let them cook for 30 seconds. 8. Transfer the cooked squash slices to a plate. Spoon the butter/herb mixture over the squash. Season with the salt and black pepper. Serve warm.

Per Serving: Calories 159; Fat 11.18g; Sodium 396mg; Carbs 15.7g; Fiber 2.6g; Sugar 0.01g; Protein 1.67g

Stewed Okra with Tomatoes

Prep Time: 5 minutes | Cook Time: 25 minutes | Serves: 4

¼ cup extra-virgin olive oil
1 large onion, chopped
4 cloves garlic, finely chopped
1 teaspoon salt
1 pound fresh or frozen okra, cleaned

1 (15-ounce) can plain tomato sauce
2 cups water
½ cup fresh cilantro, finely chopped
½ teaspoon freshly ground black pepper

1. In a large pot over medium heat, stir and cook the olive oil, onion, garlic, and salt for 1 minute. 2. Add the okra and cook for 3 minutes. 3. Add the tomato sauce, cilantro, water, and black pepper; stir, cover, and let cook for 15 minutes, stirring occasionally. 4. Serve warm.

Per Serving: Calories 200; Fat 14.18g; Sodium 602mg; Carbs 17.92g; Fiber 4.9g; Sugar 8.79g; Protein 3.87g

Spiced Cauliflower Couscous

Prep Time: 10 minutes | Cook Time: 12-14 minutes | Serves: 4

400g (14oz) cauliflower

3 tablespoons extra virgin olive oil, ghee, coconut oil or dripping

1 small onion or leek, or 5 spring onions, finely chopped

1 red pepper, cut into finger-width strips

1 fat garlic clove, finely chopped

½ teaspoon chilli flakes (optional)

1 teaspoon ground cumin

1 teaspoon ground turmeric

A small handful of coriander or flat-leaf parsley, leaves roughly chopped, stems finely chopped

Salt and freshly ground black pepper

1. Rice the cauliflower as described above and set aside. 2. Heat the fat in a wok or large frying pan. Fry the onion and pepper over medium heat for 5–7 minutes or until soft. Add the garlic, chilli, if using, cumin, turmeric and seasoning. Add the cauliflower rice along with 6 tablespoons of water. Cover and cook over a low heat for about 7 minutes or until just soft, stirring occasionally. 3. When cooked, stir in the herbs and serve straight away.

Per Serving: Calories 140; Fat 10.73g; Sodium 329mg; Carbs 10.49g; Fiber 3g; Sugar 3.46g; Protein 2.78g

Sautéed Zucchini with Garlic and Mint

Prep Time: 5 minutes | Cook Time: 10 minutes | Serves: 4

3 large green zucchini

3 tablespoons extra-virgin olive oil

1 large onion, chopped

3 cloves garlic, minced

1 teaspoon salt

1 teaspoon dried mint

1. Cut the zucchini into ½-inch cubes. 2. In a large skillet over medium heat, cook the olive oil, onions, and garlic for 3 minutes, stirring constantly. 3. Add the zucchini and salt to the skillet and toss to combine with the onions and garlic, cooking for 5 minutes. 4. Add the mint to the skillet, tossing to combine. Cook for another 2 minutes. Serve warm.

Per Serving: Calories 136; Fat 10.7g; Sodium 597mg; Carbs 9.33g; Fiber 2.3g; Sugar 5.65g; Protein 2.53g

Chapter 3 Grain and Bean Recipes

French Green Lentils with Swiss Chard

Prep Time: 15 minutes | Cook Time: 17 minutes | Serves: 6

2 tablespoons extra-virgin olive oil, plus extra for drizzling

12 ounces Swiss chard, stems chopped fine, leaves sliced into ½-inch-wide strips

1 onion, chopped fine

½ teaspoon table salt

2 garlic cloves, minced

1 teaspoon minced fresh thyme or ¼ teaspoon dried

2½ cups water

1 cup French green lentils, picked over and rinsed

3 tablespoons whole-grain mustard

½ teaspoon grated lemon zest plus 1 teaspoon juice

3 tablespoons sliced almonds, toasted

2 tablespoons chopped fresh parsley

1. Using the highest sauté function, heat the oil in the instant pot until shimmering. Add the chard stems, onion, and salt and cook for about 5 minutes, until the vegetables are softened. Stir in the garlic and thyme and cook until fragrant, about 30 seconds. Stir in the water and lentils. 2. Lock the lid in place and close the pressure release valve. Set to the high pressure cook function and cook for 11 minutes. Turn off the instant pot and let pressure release naturally for 15 minutes. Quick-release any remaining pressure, then carefully remove the lid, ensuring the steam escapes away from you. 3. Stir the chard leaves into lentils, 1 handful at a time, and let cook in residual heat until wilted, about 5 minutes. Stir in the mustard, lemon zest, and lemon juice. Season with the salt and pepper to taste. Transfer to a serving dish, drizzle with extra oil, and sprinkle with the almonds and parsley. Serve.

Per Serving: Calories 275; Fat 11.54g; Sodium 1696mg; Carbs 32.89g; Fiber 10.2g; Sugar 3.48g; Protein 14.86g

Mediterranean Veggie and Bulgur Bowl

Prep Time: 10 minutes | Cook Time: 20 minutes | Serves: 4

2 cups water

1 cup of either bulgur wheat or quinoa, rinsed

1½ teaspoons salt, divided

1 pint (2 cups) cherry tomatoes, cut in half

1 large bell pepper, chopped

1 large cucumber, chopped

1 cup Kalamata olives

½ cup freshly squeezed lemon juice

1 cup extra-virgin olive oil

½ teaspoon freshly ground black pepper

1. In a medium pot over medium heat, boil the water. Add the bulgur (or quinoa) and 1 teaspoon of salt. Cover and cook for 15 to 20 minutes. 2. To arrange the veggies in your 4 bowls, visually divide each bowl into 5 sections. Place the cooked bulgur in one section. Follow with the tomatoes, cucumbers, bell pepper, and olives. 3. In a small bowl, whisk together the lemon juice, olive oil, remaining ½ teaspoon salt, and black pepper. 4. Evenly spoon the dressing over the 4 bowls. 5. Serve immediately or cover and refrigerate for later.

Per Serving: Calories 259; Fat 9.91g; Sodium 1130mg; Carbs 37.14g; Fiber 5.8g; Sugar 4.27g; Protein 7.71g

Greek Chickpeas with Herbs

Prep Time: 20 minutes | Cook Time: 22 minutes | Serves: 6-8

1½ tablespoons table salt, for brining

1 pound (2½ cups) dried chickpeas, picked over and rinsed

2 tablespoons extra-virgin olive oil, plus extra for drizzling

2 onions, halved and sliced thin

¼ teaspoon table salt

1 tablespoon coriander seeds, cracked

¼–½ teaspoon red pepper flakes

2½ cups chicken broth

¼ cup fresh sage leaves

2 bay leaves

1½ teaspoons grated lemon zest plus 2 teaspoons juice

2 tablespoons minced fresh parsley

1. Dissolve 1½ tablespoons salt in 2 quarts cold water in a large container. Add the chickpeas and soak at room temperature for at least 8 hours or up to 24 hours. Drain and rinse well. 2. Using the highest sauté function, heat the oil in the instant pot until shimmering. Add the onions and ¼ teaspoon salt and cook until the onions are softened and well browned, 10 to 12 minutes. Stir in the coriander and pepper flakes and cook until fragrant, about 30 seconds. Stir in the broth, scraping up any browned bits, then stir in the chickpeas, sage, and bay leaves. 3. Lock the lid in place and close the pressure release valve. Select low pressure cook function and cook for 10 minutes. Turn off the instant pot and let pressure release naturally for 15 minutes. Quick-release any remaining pressure, then carefully remove the lid, ensuring the steam escapes away from you. 4. Discard the bay leaves. Stir the lemon zest and juice into chickpeas and season with the salt and pepper to taste. Sprinkle with the parsley. Serve, drizzling individual portions with extra oil.

Per Serving: Calories 291; Fat 8.2g; Sodium 1925mg; Carbs 42.48g; Fiber 8.6g; Sugar 7.49g; Protein 14.07g

Bulgur with Chickpeas and Spinach

Prep Time: 15 minutes | Cook Time: 7 minutes | Serves: 4-6

3 tablespoons extra-virgin olive oil, divided

1 onion, chopped fine

½ teaspoon table salt

3 garlic cloves, minced

2 tablespoons za'atar, divided

1 cup medium-grind bulgur, rinsed

1 (15-ounce) can chickpeas, rinsed

1½ cups water

5 ounces (5 cups) baby spinach, chopped

1 tablespoon lemon juice, plus lemon wedges for serving

1. Using the highest sauté function, heat 2 tablespoons oil in the instant pot until shimmering. Add the onion and salt and cook until the onion is softened, about 5 minutes. Stir in the garlic and 1 tablespoon za'atar and cook until fragrant, about 30 seconds. Stir in the bulgur, chickpeas, and water. 2. Lock the lid in place and close the pressure release valve. Set to the high pressure cook function and cook for 1 minute. Turn off the instant pot and quickly release pressure. Carefully remove the lid, ensuring the steam escapes away from you. 3. Gently fluff the bulgur with a fork. Lay clean dish towel over the pot, replace the lid, and allow to sit for 5 minutes. Add the spinach, remaining 1 tablespoon za'atar, lemon juice, and remaining 1 tablespoon oil and gently toss to combine. Season with the salt and pepper to taste. Serve with the lemon wedges.

Per Serving: Calories 257; Fat 10.03g; Sodium 387mg; Carbs 36.62g; Fiber 7.8g; Sugar 3.32g; Protein 8.19g

Lemony Avocado Farro Bowl

Prep Time: 5 minutes | Cook Time: 25 minutes | Serves: 6

1 tablespoon plus 2 teaspoons extra-virgin olive oil, divided

1 cup chopped onion (about ½ medium onion)

2 garlic cloves, minced (about 1 teaspoon)

1 carrot, shredded (about 1 cup)

2 cups low-sodium or no-salt-added vegetable broth

1 cup (6 ounces) uncooked pearled or 10-minute farro

2 avocados, peeled, pitted, and sliced

1 small lemon

¼ teaspoon kosher or sea salt

1. In a medium saucepan over medium-high heat, heat 1 tablespoon of oil. Add the onion and cook for 5 minutes, stirring occasionally. Add the garlic and carrot and cook for 1 minute, stirring frequently. Add the broth and farro, and bring to a boil over high heat. Lower the heat to medium-low, cover, and simmer for about 20 minutes or until the farro is plump and slightly chewy (al dente). 2. Pour the farro into a serving bowl, and add the avocado slices. Using a Microplane or citrus zester, zest the peel of the lemon directly into the bowl of farro. Cut the lemon in half, and squeeze the juice out of both halves using a citrus juicer or your hands. Drizzle the remaining 2 teaspoons of oil over the bowl, and sprinkle with salt. Gently mix all the ingredients and serve.

Per Serving: Calories 249; Fat 11.03g; Sodium 113mg; Carbs 35.97g; Fiber 10.5g; Sugar 2.53g; Protein 5.12g

Lemon Fava and Garbanzo Bean

Prep Time: 10 minutes | Cook Time: 10 minutes | Serves: 6

1 (16-ounce) can garbanzo beans, rinsed and drained

1 (15-ounce) can fava beans, rinsed and drained

3 cups water

½ cup lemon juice

3 cloves garlic, peeled and minced

1 teaspoon salt

3 tablespoons extra-virgin olive oil

1. In a 3-quart pot over medium heat, cook the garbanzo beans, fava beans, and water for 10 minutes. 2. Reserving 1 cup of the liquid from the cooked beans, drain the beans and put them in a bowl. 3. Mix the reserved liquid, lemon juice, minced garlic, and salt together and add to the beans in the bowl. Using a potato masher, mash up about half the beans in the bowl. 4. After mashing half the beans, give the mixture one more stir to make sure the beans are evenly mixed. 5. Drizzle the olive oil over the top. 6. Serve warm or cold with pita bread.

Per Serving: Calories 161; Fat 7.59g; Sodium 485mg; Carbs 19.75g; Fiber 4.3g; Sugar 5.75g; Protein 7.32g

Mediterranean Lentils and Brown Rice

Prep Time: 5 minutes | Cook Time: 25 minutes | Serves: 4

2¼ cups low-sodium or no-salt-added vegetable broth

½ cup uncooked brown or green lentils

½ cup uncooked instant brown rice

½ cup diced carrots (about 1 carrot)

½ cup diced celery (about 1 stalk)

1 (2.25-ounce) can sliced olives, drained (about ½ cup)

¼ cup diced red onion (about ⅛ onion)

¼ cup chopped fresh curly-leaf parsley

1½ tablespoons extra-virgin olive oil

1 tablespoon freshly squeezed lemon juice (from about ½ small lemon)

1 garlic clove, minced (about ½ teaspoon)

¼ teaspoon kosher or sea salt

¼ teaspoon freshly ground black pepper

1. In a medium saucepan over high heat, bring the broth and lentils to a boil, cover, and lower the heat to medium-low. Cook for 8 minutes. 2. Raise the heat to medium, and stir in the rice. Cover the pot and cook the mixture for 15 minutes, or until the liquid is absorbed. Remove the pot from the heat and let it sit, covered, for 1 minute, then stir. 3. While the lentils and rice are cooking, mix together the carrots, olives, onion, celery, and parsley in a large serving bowl. 4. In a small bowl, whisk together the oil, garlic, salt, lemon juice, and pepper. Set aside. 5. When finished, add the lentils and rice to the serving bowl. Pour the dressing over the lentils and rice and mix everything together. Serve warm or cold, or store in a sealed container in the refrigerator for up to 7 days.

Per Serving: Calories 259; Fat 8.55g; Sodium 943mg; Carbs 38.57g; Fiber 4.7g; Sugar 3.16g; Protein 8.36g

Lentils and Bulgur with Caramelized Onions

Prep Time: 10 minutes | Cook Time: 50 minutes | Serves: 6

½ cup extra-virgin olive oil

4 large onions, chopped

2 teaspoons salt, divided

6 cups water

2 cups brown lentils, picked over and rinsed

1 teaspoon freshly ground black pepper

1 cup bulgur wheat

1. In a large pot over medium heat, cook and stir the olive oil, onions, and 1 teaspoon of salt for 12 to 15 minutes, until the onions are a medium brown/golden color. 2. Put half of the cooked onions in a bowl. 3. Add the water, remaining 1 teaspoon of salt, and lentils to the remaining onions. Stir. Cover and cook for 30 minutes. 4. Stir in the black pepper and bulgur, cover, and cook for 5 minutes. Fluff with a fork, cover, and let stand for another 5 minutes. 5. Spoon the lentils and bulgur onto a serving plate and top with the reserved onions. Serve warm.

Per Serving: Calories 333; Fat 22.6g; Sodium 930mg; Carbs 27.46g; Fiber 8g; Sugar 5.37g; Protein 7.56g

Bulgur and Garbanzo Bean Pilaf

Prep Time: 5 minutes | Cook Time: 20 minutes | Serves: 4-6

3 tablespoons extra-virgin olive oil

1 large onion, chopped

1 (16-ounce) can garbanzo beans, rinsed and drained

2 cups bulgur wheat, rinsed and drained

1½ teaspoons salt

½ teaspoon cinnamon

4 cups water

1. In a large pot over medium heat, cook the olive oil and onion for 5 minutes. 2. Add the garbanzo beans and cook for an additional 5 minutes. 3. Add the bulgur, cinnamon, salt, and water and stir to combine. Cover the pot, turn the heat to low, and cook for 10 minutes. 4. When the cooking is done, fluff the pilaf with a fork. Cover and let sit for another 5 minutes.

Per Serving: Calories 224; Fat 8.97g; Sodium 851mg; Carbs 30.67g; Fiber 3.9g; Sugar 1.35g; Protein 7.37g

Homemade Cuban Black Beans

Prep Time: 10 minutes | Cook Time: 57-74 minutes | Serves: 8

Salt and pepper

1 pound dried black beans (2½ cups) picked over and rinsed

2 slices bacon, chopped fine

2 onions, chopped

1 red bell pepper, stemmed, seeded, and chopped

1 teaspoon ground cumin

6 garlic cloves, minced

2 teaspoons minced fresh oregano or ¾ teaspoon dried

¼ teaspoon red pepper flakes

3½ cups water

2 bay leaves

⅛ teaspoon baking soda

¼ cup minced fresh cilantro

1 tablespoon lime juice

1. Dissolve 1½ tablespoons salt in 2 quarts cold water in a large container. Add the beans and soak at room temperature for at least 8 hours or up to 1 day. Drain and rinse well. 2. Adjust the oven rack to lower-middle position and heat the oven to 300 degrees. In a Dutch oven over medium heat, cook the bacon until crisp, 5 to 7 minutes. Stir in the onions, cumin, bell pepper, and ½ teaspoon salt and cook until softened, 5 to 7 minutes. Stir in the oregano, garlic, and red pepper flakes and cook until fragrant, about 30 seconds. Stir in water, scraping up any browned bits. Stir in the bay leaves, beans, and baking soda and bring to simmer. 3. Cover, transfer the pot to oven, and bake, stirring every 30 minutes, until the beans are tender, about 1½ hours. Remove the lid and continue to bake until the liquid has thickened, 15 to 30 minutes, stirring halfway through cooking. 4. Discard the bay leaves. Let the beans sit for 10 minutes. Stir in the cilantro and lime juice. Season with the pepper to taste and serve.

Per Serving: Calories 240; Fat 3.53g; Sodium 350mg; Carbs 40.02g; Fiber 9.7g; Sugar 2.8g; Protein 13.75g

Spiced Quinoa with Almonds

Prep Time: 15 minutes | Cook Time: 0 minute | Serves: 4

2 cups cooked quinoa

⅓ teaspoon cranberries or currants

¼ cup sliced almonds

2 garlic cloves, minced

1¼ teaspoons salt

½ teaspoon ground cumin

½ teaspoon turmeric

¼ teaspoon ground cinnamon

¼ teaspoon freshly ground black pepper

1. In a large bowl, toss the quinoa, cranberries, garlic, salt, cumin, almonds, turmeric, cinnamon, and pepper and stir to combine. Enjoy alone or with roasted cauliflower.

Per Serving: Calories 150; Fat 4.74g; Sodium 734mg; Carbs 22.08g; Fiber 3.6g; Sugar 1.11g; Protein 5.49g

Mediterranean Farro Bowl

Prep Time: 15 minutes | Cook Time: 10 minutes | Serves: 4-6

⅓ cup extra-virgin olive oil

½ cup chopped red bell pepper

⅓ cup chopped red onions

2 garlic cloves, minced

1 cup zucchini, cut in ½-inch slices

½ cup canned chickpeas, drained and rinsed

½ cup coarsely chopped artichokes

3 cups cooked farro

Salt

Freshly ground black pepper

¼ cup sliced olives, for serving (optional)

2 tablespoons fresh basil, chiffonade, for serving (optional)

3 tablespoons balsamic reduction, for serving (optional)

1. In a large sauté pan or skillet, heat the oil over medium heat and sauté the pepper, onions, and garlic for about 5 minutes, until tender. 2. Add the chickpeas, zucchini, and artichokes, then stir and continue to sauté the vegetables, approximately 5 more minutes, until just soft. 3. Stir in the cooked farro, tossing to combine and cooking enough to heat through. Season with the salt and pepper and remove from the heat. 4. Transfer the contents of the pan into the serving vessels or bowls. 5. Top with the olives and basil (if using). Drizzle with the balsamic reduction (if using) to finish.

Per Serving: Calories 327; Fat 17.72g; Sodium 540mg; Carbs 35.41g; Fiber 6.1g; Sugar 4.55g; Protein 8.08g

Barley with Mint and Cilantro

Prep Time: 15 minutes | Cook Time: 30-52 minutes | Serves: 6

1½ cups pearled barley

Salt and pepper

3 tablespoons extra-virgin olive oil

1 teaspoon grated lemon zest plus 3 tablespoons juice

¼ cup minced fresh cilantro

2 tablespoons minced shallot

1 teaspoon Dijon mustard

6 scallions, sliced thin on bias

¼ cup minced fresh mint

1. Bring 4 quarts water to boil in a large pot. Add the barley and 1 teaspoon salt and cook, adjusting heat to maintain gentle boil, until the barley is tender with slight chew, 25 to 45 minutes. 2. Meanwhile, whisk the oil, lemon zest and juice, mustard, ¼ teaspoon salt, shallot, and ½ teaspoon pepper in large bowl. 3. Drain the barley well. Transfer to a parchment paper–lined rimmed baking sheet and spread into even layer. Let sit until no longer steaming, 5 to 7 minutes. Add the barley to the bowl with dressing and toss to coat. Add the scallions, mint, and cilantro and gently toss to combine. Season with the pepper to taste. Serve.

Per Serving: Calories 247; Fat 7.43g; Sodium 405mg; Carbs 41.57g; Fiber 8.6g; Sugar 1.23g; Protein 5.47g

Herbed Lentil Rice Balls

Prep Time: 5 minutes | Cook Time: 11 minutes | Serves: 6

½ cup cooked green lentils

2 garlic cloves, minced

¼ white onion, minced

¼ cup parsley leaves

5 basil leaves

1 cup cooked brown rice

1 tablespoon lemon juice

1 tablespoon olive oil

½ teaspoon salt

1. Preheat the air fryer to 380°F. 2. In a food processor, pulse the cooked lentils with the garlic, parsley, onion, and basil until mostly smooth. (You will want some bits of lentils in the mixture.) 3. Pour the lentil mixture into a large bowl, and stir in brown rice, olive oil, lemon juice, and salt. Stir until well combined. 4. Form the rice mixture into 1-inch balls. Place the rice balls in a single layer in the air fryer basket, making sure that they don't touch each other. 5. Fry for 6 minutes. Turn the rice balls and then fry for an additional 4 to 5 minutes, or until browned on all sides.

Per Serving: Calories 117; Fat 2.73g; Sodium 197mg; Carbs 18.88g; Fiber 2.5g; Sugar 0.73g; Protein 4.91g

Herbed White Bean Casserole

Prep Time: 5 minutes | Cook Time: 15 minutes | Serves: 4

Olive oil cooking spray

2 (15-ounce) cans white beans, or cannellini beans, drained and rinsed

1 red bell pepper, diced

½ red onion, diced

3 garlic cloves, minced

1 tablespoon olive oil

¼ to ½ teaspoon salt

½ teaspoon black pepper

1 rosemary sprig

1 bay leaf

1. Preheat the air fryer to 360°F. Lightly coat the inside of a 5-cup capacity casserole dish with olive oil cooking spray. (The shape of the casserole dish will depend upon the size of the air fryer, but it needs to be able to hold at least 5 cups.) 2. In a large bowl, combine the beans, bell pepper, salt, onion, garlic, olive oil, and pepper. 3. Pour the bean mixture into the prepared casserole dish, place the rosemary and bay leaf on top, and then place the casserole dish into the air fryer. 4. Roast for 15 minutes. 5. Remove the rosemary and bay leaves, then stir well before serving.

Per Serving: Calories 299; Fat 5.66g; Sodium 599mg; Carbs 48.44g; Fiber 1.1g; Sugar 1.86g; Protein 15.62g

Brown Rice with Tomatoes and Chickpeas

Prep Time: 15 minutes | Cook Time: 57-65 minutes | Serves: 8

12 ounces grape tomatoes, quartered

5 scallions, sliced thin

¼ cup minced fresh cilantro

4 teaspoons extra-virgin olive oil

1 tablespoon lime juice

Salt and pepper

2 red bell peppers, stemmed, seeded, and chopped fine

1 onion, chopped fine

1 cup long-grain brown rice, rinsed

4 garlic cloves, minced

Pinch saffron threads, crumbled

Pinch cayenne pepper

3¼ cups unsalted chicken broth

1 (15-ounce) can no-salt-added chickpeas, rinsed

1. Combine the tomatoes, 2 teaspoons oil, lime juice, ⅛ teaspoon salt, scallions, cilantro, and ⅛ teaspoon pepper in a bowl; set aside for serving. 2. Heat the remaining 2 teaspoons oil in a 12-inch skillet over medium heat until shimmering. Add the bell peppers, onion, and ¼ teaspoon salt and cook until softened and lightly browned, 8 to 10 minutes. Stir in the rice, garlic, saffron, and cayenne and cook until fragrant, about 30 seconds. 3. Stir in the broth, scraping up any browned bits, and bring to simmer. Reduce heat to medium-low, cover, and cook, stirring occasionally, for 25 minutes. 4. Stir in the chickpeas and ⅛ teaspoon salt, cover, and cook until the rice is tender and broth is almost completely absorbed, 25 to 30 minutes. Season with the pepper to taste. Serve, topping individual portions with tomato mixture.

Per Serving: Calories 226; Fat 4.73g; Sodium 678mg; Carbs 39.04g; Fiber 6.3g; Sugar 6.03g; Protein 8.33g

Chapter 4 Snack and Appetizer Recipes

Spicy Garlic Shrimp

Prep Time: 15 minutes | Cook Time: 5 minutes | Serves: 6

½ cup olive oil

5 cloves garlic, minced

1 teaspoon red pepper flakes

24 large shrimp, peeled and deveined

Juice and zest from 1 lemon

Sea salt and freshly ground pepper, to taste

1. Heat the olive oil in a large skillet over medium-high heat. Add the garlic and red pepper flakes, and cook for 1 minute. 2. Add the shrimp and cook for another 3 minutes, stirring frequently. Remove from the pan, and sprinkle with lemon juice, sea salt, and pepper.
Per Serving: Calories 186; Fat 18.37g; Sodium 353mg; Carbs 1.93g; Fiber 0.2g; Sugar 0.26g; Protein 4.05g

Lemony Roasted Asparagus

Prep Time: 5 minutes | Cook Time: 15 minutes | Serves: 4

1 pound asparagus, ends trimmed

2 tablespoons extra-virgin olive oil

Juice and grated zest of ½ lemon

¼ teaspoon salt

¼ teaspoon freshly ground black pepper

1. Preheat the oven to 400°F. Line a baking sheet with a silicone baking mat or aluminum foil. 2. Place the asparagus on the prepared baking sheet and drizzle with the olive oil, rubbing to fully coat all the spears. 3. Sprinkle with the lemon juice, salt, lemon zest, and pepper. Lightly toss the asparagus to distribute the toppings, then evenly space the spears across the baking sheet. 4. Bake for 12 to 15 minutes, or until tender-crisp. Serve immediately. Store any leftovers in an airtight container in the refrigerator for up to 4 days.
Per Serving: Calories 84; Fat 6.91g; Sodium 148mg; Carbs 4.91g; Fiber 2.4g; Sugar 2.28g; Protein 2.53g

Salmon Stuffed Cucumbers

Prep Time: 10 minutes | Cook Time: 0 minute | Serves: 4

2 large cucumbers, peeled

1 (4-ounce) can red salmon

1 medium very ripe avocado, peeled, pitted, and mashed

1 tablespoon extra-virgin olive oil

Zest and juice of 1 lime

3 tablespoons chopped fresh cilantro

½ teaspoon salt

¼ teaspoon freshly ground black pepper

1. Slice the cucumber into 1-inch-thick segments and using a spoon, scrape seeds out of center of each segment and stand up on a plate. 2. In a medium bowl, combine the salmon, avocado, lime zest and juice, cilantro, salt, olive oil, and pepper and mix until creamy. 3. Spoon the salmon mixture into the center of each cucumber segment and serve chilled.
Per Serving: Calories 177; Fat 12.67g; Sodium 407mg; Carbs 9.2g; Fiber 4.9g; Sugar 2.55g; Protein 9.44g

Citrus Marinated Olives

Prep Time: 10 minutes | Cook Time: 0 minute | Serves: 4

2 cups mixed green olives with pits
¼ cup red wine vinegar
¼ cup extra-virgin olive oil
4 garlic cloves, finely minced
Zest and juice of 2 clementines or 1 large orange

1 teaspoon red pepper flakes
2 bay leaves
½ teaspoon ground cumin
½ teaspoon ground allspice

1. In a large glass bowl or jar, combine the olives, garlic, orange zest and juice, vinegar, oil, red pepper flakes, cumin, bay leaves, and allspice and mix well. Cover and refrigerate for at least 4 hours or up to a week to allow the olives to marinate, tossing again before serving.
Per Serving: Calories 167; Fat 13.87g; Sodium 164mg; Carbs 9.95g; Fiber 2.9g; Sugar 3.47g; Protein 2.49g

Creamy Hummus

Prep Time: 5 minutes | Cook Time: 0 minute | Serves: 8

1 (15-ounce) can garbanzo beans, rinsed and drained
2 cloves garlic, peeled
¼ cup lemon juice
1 teaspoon salt

¼ cup plain Greek yogurt
½ cup tahini paste
2 tablespoons extra-virgin olive oil, divided

1. Add the garbanzo beans, garlic cloves, lemon juice, and salt to a food processor fitted with a chopping blade. Blend for 1 minute, until smooth. 2. Scrape down the sides of the processor. Add the Greek yogurt, tahini paste, and 1 tablespoon of olive oil and blend for another minute, until creamy and well combined. 3. Spoon the hummus into a serving bowl and drizzle the remaining tablespoon of olive oil on top.
Per Serving: Calories 187; Fat 11.72g; Sodium 311mg; Carbs 15.32g; Fiber 5.2g; Sugar 0.41g; Protein 7.5g

Mediterranean Trail Mix

Prep Time: 5 minutes | Cook Time: 0 minute | Serves: 6

1 cup roughly chopped unsalted walnuts
½ cup roughly chopped salted almonds
½ cup shelled salted pistachios

½ cup roughly chopped apricots
½ cup roughly chopped dates
⅓ cup dried figs, sliced in half

1. In a large zip-top bag, combine the walnuts, pistachios, almonds, apricots, dates, and figs and mix well.
Per Serving: Calories 335; Fat 23.53g; Sodium 104mg; Carbs 29.24g; Fiber 6.1g; Sugar 19.34g; Protein 8.47g

Crunchy Orange Chickpeas

Prep Time: 5 minutes | Cook Time: 20 minutes | Serves: 4

1 (15-ounce) can chickpeas, drained and rinsed

2 teaspoons extra-virgin olive oil

¼ teaspoon dried thyme or ½ teaspoon chopped fresh thyme

leaves

⅛ teaspoon kosher or sea salt

Zest of ½ orange (about ½ teaspoon)

1. Preheat the oven to 450°F. 2. Spread the chickpeas on a clean kitchen towel, and rub gently until dry. 3. Lay the chickpeas on a large, rimmed baking sheet. Drizzle with the oil, and sprinkle with the thyme and salt. Using a Microplane or citrus zester, zest about half of the orange over the chickpeas. Mix well using your hands. 4. Bake for 10 minutes, then open the oven door and, using an oven mitt, give the baking sheet a quick shake. (Do not remove the sheet from the oven.) Bake for 10 minutes more. Taste the chickpeas (carefully!). If they are golden but you think they could be a bit crunchier, bake for 3 minutes more before serving.

Per Serving: Calories 108; Fat 3.82g; Sodium 212mg; Carbs 14.63g; Fiber 4.1g; Sugar 2.54g; Protein 4.48g

Air Fryer Sea Salt Beet Chips

Prep Time: 10 minutes | Cook Time: 30 minutes | Serves: 6

4 medium beets, rinse and sliced thin

1 teaspoon sea salt

2 tablespoons olive oil

Hummus, for serving

1. Preheat the air fryer to 380°F. 2. In a large bowl, toss the beets with the sea salt and olive oil until well coated. 3. Put the beet slices into the air fryer and spread them out in a single layer. 4. Fry for 10 minutes. Stir, then fry for an additional 10 minutes. Stir again, then fry for a final 5 to 10 minutes, or until the chips reach the desired crispiness. 5. Serve with a favorite hummus.

Per Serving: Calories 68; Fat 4.81g; Sodium 436mg; Carbs 5.73g; Fiber 1.6g; Sugar 3.7g; Protein 1g

Garlic Butter Sautéed Mushrooms

Prep Time: 10 minutes | Cook Time: 10 minutes | Serves: 4-6

2 pounds cremini mushrooms, cleaned

3 tablespoons unsalted butter

2 tablespoons garlic, minced

½ teaspoon salt

½ teaspoon freshly ground black pepper

1. Cut each mushroom in half, stem to top, and put them into a bowl. 2. Preheat a large sauté pan or skillet over medium heat. 3. Cook the butter and garlic in the pan for 2 minutes, stirring occasionally. 4. Add the mushrooms and salt to the pan and toss together with the garlic butter mixture. Cook for 7 to 8 minutes, stirring every 2 minutes. 5. Remove the mushrooms from the pan and pour into a serving dish. Top with the black pepper.

Per Serving: Calories 109; Fat 5.54g; Sodium 253mg; Carbs 13.6g; Fiber 4.7g; Sugar 4.35g; Protein 4.58g

Baked Kale Chips

Prep Time: 5 minutes | Cook Time: 10 to 15 minutes | Serves: 4

2 heads curly leaf kale

2 tablespoons olive oil

Sea salt, to taste

1. Tear the kale into bite-sized pieces. 2. Toss with the olive oil, and lay on a baking sheet in a single layer. Sprinkle with a pinch of sea salt. 3. Bake for 10–15 minutes until crispy. Serve or store in an airtight container.

Per Serving: Calories 115; Fat 7.8g; Sodium 334mg; Carbs 9.92g; Fiber 4.1g; Sugar 2.56g; Protein 4.85g

Zesty Artichoke Antipasto

Prep Time: 10 minutes | Cook Time: 0 minute | Serves: 4

1 (12-ounce) jar roasted red peppers, drained, stemmed, and seeded

8 artichoke hearts, either frozen (thawed), or jarred (drained)

1 (16-ounce) can garbanzo beans, drained

1 cup whole Kalamata olives, drained

¼ cup balsamic vinegar

½ teaspoon salt

1. Cut the peppers into ½-inch slices and put them into a large bowl. 2. Cut the artichoke hearts into quarters, and add them to the bowl. 3. Add the garbanzo beans, balsamic vinegar, olives, and salt. 4. Toss all the ingredients together. Serve chilled.

Per Serving: Calories 225; Fat 4.37g; Sodium 764mg; Carbs 37.52g; Fiber 12.6g; Sugar 6.42g; Protein 11.46g

Smoky Baba Ghanoush

Prep Time: 50 minutes | Cook Time: 40 minutes | Serves: 6

2 large eggplants, washed

¼ cup lemon juice

1 teaspoon garlic, minced

1 teaspoon salt

½ cup tahini paste

3 tablespoons extra-virgin olive oil

1. Grill the whole eggplants over a low flame using a gas stovetop or grill. Rotate the eggplant every 5 minutes to make sure that all sides are cooked evenly. Continue to do this for 40 minutes. 2. Remove the eggplants from the stove or grill and put them onto a plate or into a bowl; cover with plastic wrap. Let sit for 5 to 10 minutes. 3. Using your fingers, peel away and discard the charred skin of the eggplants. Cut off the stem. 4. Put the eggplants into a food processor fitted with a chopping blade. Add the lemon juice, salt, garlic, and tahini paste, and pulse the mixture 5 to 7 times. 5. Pour the eggplant mixture onto a serving plate. Drizzle with the olive oil. Serve chilled or at room temperature.

Per Serving: Calories 220; Fat 17.8g; Sodium 414mg; Carbs 14.07g; Fiber 6.5g; Sugar 5.75g; Protein 4.96g

Healthy Corn, Avocado, and Tomato Medley

Prep Time: 15 minutes | Cook Time: 0 minute | Serves: 6

1 (15-ounce) can corn, drained and rinsed

1 (14½-ounce) can no-salt-added diced tomatoes, drained

1 (10-ounce) can diced tomatoes with lime juice and cilantro, drained

1 large avocado, peeled, pitted, and diced

½ medium red onion, diced

¼ cup packed chopped fresh cilantro

1 tablespoon extra-virgin olive oil

1 teaspoon grated lime zest

1 teaspoon freshly squeezed lime juice

½ teaspoon salt

¼ teaspoon freshly ground black pepper

1. In a large bowl, stir the corn, tomatoes, cilantro, olive oil, lime zest, avocado, red onion, salt, lime juice, and pepper until well combined. 2. Serve right away, or cover and place in the refrigerator for at least 30 minutes to let the flavors combine and develop. Store any leftovers, covered, in the refrigerator for up to 5 days.

Per Serving: Calories 147; Fat 8.44g; Sodium 340mg; Carbs 18.63g; Fiber 6.3g; Sugar 5.31g; Protein 3.36g

Sautéed Zucchini Ribbons with Cherry Tomatoes

Prep Time: 10 minutes | Cook Time: 10 minutes | Serves: 4

1 medium zucchini

1 tablespoon extra-virgin olive oil

½ medium yellow onion, diced

1 cup halved cherry tomatoes

2 garlic cloves, minced

¼ teaspoon salt

⅛ teaspoon freshly ground black pepper

1 tablespoon freshly squeezed lemon juice

1 teaspoon grated lemon zest

1. Use a vegetable peeler or mandoline to slice the zucchini lengthwise into thin ribbons. 2. In a large skillet, heat the olive oil over medium heat. Add the zucchini and onion and cook until they start to soften, 3 to 5 minutes. Add the tomatoes, salt, garlic, and pepper and cook until the zucchini is tender-crisp and the tomatoes have started to collapse, about 5 minutes. 3. Stir in the lemon juice and cook for 1 more minute. Transfer to a serving dish and garnish with the lemon zest; serve hot. Refrigerate any leftovers in an airtight container for up to 5 days.

Per Serving: Calories 51; Fat 3.6g; Sodium 149mg; Carbs 4.5g; Fiber 1.1g; Sugar 1.7g; Protein 1.37g

Spicy Roasted Red Potatoes

Prep Time: 20 minutes | Cook Time: 25 minutes | Serves: 5

1½ pounds red potatoes or gold potatoes

3 tablespoons garlic, minced

1½ teaspoons salt

¼ cup extra-virgin olive oil

½ cup fresh cilantro, chopped

½ teaspoon freshly ground black pepper

¼ teaspoon cayenne pepper

3 tablespoons lemon juice

1. Preheat the oven to 450°F. 2. Scrub the potatoes and pat dry. 3. Cut the potatoes into ½-inch pieces and put them into a bowl. 4. Add the salt, garlic, and olive oil and toss everything together to evenly coat. 5. Pour the potato mixture onto a baking sheet, spread the potatoes out evenly, and put them into the oven, roasting for 25 minutes. Halfway through roasting, turn the potatoes with a spatula; continue roasting for the remainder of time until the potato edges start to brown. 6. Remove the potatoes from the oven and allow them to cool on the baking sheet for 5 minutes. 7. Using a spatula, remove the potatoes from the pan and put them into a bowl. 8. Add the cilantro, cayenne, black pepper, and lemon juice to the potatoes and toss until well mixed. 9. Serve warm.

Per Serving: Calories 202; Fat 11.07g; Sodium 724mg; Carbs 24.22g; Fiber 2.6g; Sugar 2.06g; Protein 3g

Chili Lime Popcorn

Prep Time: 5 minutes | Cook Time: 10 minutes | Serves: 8

1 tablespoon avocado oil

½ cup popcorn kernels

2 teaspoons chili powder

½ teaspoon salt

¼ teaspoon garlic powder

1 lime

1. In a large, heavy saucepan, heat the avocado oil over medium heat. Add the popcorn kernels and cover with a lid. 2. Reduce the heat and shake the pan occasionally, helping all the kernels pop and preventing burning the already-popped kernels, 6 to 7 minutes. When the popping slows, remove the pan from the heat, still covered, and allow the popcorn to slightly cool. 3. Transfer the popcorn to a large bowl, discarding any kernels that did not pop. Sprinkle the chili powder, salt, and garlic powder over the popcorn, and grate the zest of the lime over the top. Lightly toss it to ensure the popcorn is evenly coated. Right before serving, cut the lime in half and squeeze the fresh juice over the popcorn, tossing to coat.

Per Serving: Calories 31; Fat 1.98g; Sodium 165mg; Carbs 3.15g; Fiber 0.5g; Sugar 0.44g; Protein 0.45g

Chapter 5 Poultry Recipes

Italian Herb Grilled Chicken

Prep Time: 20 minutes | Cook Time: 10 minutes | Serves: 4

½ cup lemon juice

½ cup extra-virgin olive oil

3 tablespoons garlic, minced

2 teaspoons dried oregano

1 teaspoon red pepper flakes

1 teaspoon salt

2 pounds boneless and skinless chicken breasts

1. In a large bowl, mix together the lemon juice, garlic, oregano, olive oil, red pepper flakes, and salt. 2. Fillet the chicken breast in half horizontally to get 2 thin pieces, repeating with all of the breasts. 3. Put the chicken in the bowl with the marinade and let sit for at least 10 minutes before cooking. 4. Preheat a grill, grill pan, or lightly oiled skillet to high heat. Once hot, cook the chicken for 4 minutes on each side. Serve warm.

Per Serving: Calories 505; Fat 30.9g; Sodium 699mg; Carbs 4.81g; Fiber 0.6g; Sugar 0.9g; Protein 50.96g

Mustard Roasted Chicken with Steamed Vegetables

Prep Time: 5 minutes | Cook Time: 20 minutes | Serves: 2

1 onion, finely sliced into half-moons

3 tablespoons extra virgin olive oil

4 tablespoons water

2 sprigs of rosemary

2 tablespoons English mustard

2 medium skinless chicken breasts

Salt and freshly ground black pepper

1. Preheat the oven to 220°C/200°C fan/425°F/gas mark 7. 2. Toss the onion with 2 tablespoons of the oil and some seasoning, then divide into 2 piles in an ovenproof dish. Pour over the water and lay a rosemary sprig on each pile. 3. Spoon the mustard into a separate bowl so you aren't going back and forth between the uncooked chicken and the pot. Spread the mustard over both breasts with the back of the spoon. Lay them on top of the onion. Drizzle over the remaining oil and grind over a little pepper. 4. Cook for 20 minutes or until the chicken is cooked through and pink juices no longer run from the chicken when the thickest part is pierced with a fork. Thicker breasts may take longer to cook. You can also use a probe thermometer to make sure it is at 74°C (165°F) inside. 5. To make a parcel for the steamed vegetables, cut a piece of baking parchment at least 10cm (4in) larger than the food you are about to cook. Lay the vegetables, seasoning, any oil or butter and herbs or spices in the center of the parchment. Fold the long ends up to meet each other above the food. Make a fold of both pieces together of about 2cm (¾in) then fold again. Repeat until the fold is about 4cm (1½in) above the food. Now twist each end like a sweet wrapper. Transfer to a baking tray. 6. The vegetables will take 7–15 minutes depending on their density and size. The more watery, soft vegetables, such as zucchini, take less time than firm carrots, and the finer you cut them, the quicker they will cook. You can press the top of the parcel(s) to feel the give in the vegetables. 7. Serve your choice of steamed vegetables in the parcel alongside the mustard chicken.

Per Serving: Calories 400; Fat 24.94g; Sodium 841mg; Carbs 6.57g; Fiber 1.8g; Sugar 2.48g; Protein 36.48g

Turkey and Butternut Squash Ragout

Prep Time: 15 minutes | Cook Time: 7 to 8 hours | Serves: 4

1½ lb turkey thighs (about 2 medium), skin removed

1 small butternut squash (about 2 lb), peeled, seeded, cut into 1½-inch pieces (3 cups)

1 medium onion, cut in half, then cut into slices

1 can (16 oz) baked beans, undrained

1 can (14.5 oz) diced tomatoes with Italian herbs, undrained

2 tablespoons chopped fresh parsley

1. Spray 3- to 4-quart slow cooker with cooking spray. In the slow cooker, mix all ingredients except parsley. 2. Cover; cook on Low heat setting for 7 to 8 hours. 3. Transfer the turkey from slow cooker to a cutting board. Remove the meat from bones; discard bones. Return the turkey to the slow cooker and stir to reheat. Just before serving, sprinkle with the parsley.

Per Serving: Calories 442; Fat 7.71g; Sodium 346mg; Carbs 47.71g; Fiber 14.1g; Sugar 9.26g; Protein 48.78g

Rosemary Roasted Chicken with Chilli Sauce

Prep Time: 5 minutes | Cook Time: 20-25 minutes | Serves: 6

2 tablespoons extra virgin olive oil

3 rosemary sprigs, halved

12 boneless and skinless chicken thighs

2 onions, cut into 8 wedges

2 red bell or Romano peppers

2 zucchini or 1 eggplant or 1 small head of broccoli

2 handfuls of watercress, rocket or lettuce

Salt and freshly ground black pepper

1 lemon, cut into wedges, to serve

For the Chilli Sauce:

1–2 red chillies, depending on strength, or ½ teaspoon chilli flakes

2 garlic cloves

6 tablespoons olive oil

1 sprig of rosemary, stem discarded

¼ teaspoon salt and plenty of freshly ground black pepper

1. Preheat the oven to 220°C/200°C fan/475°F/gas mark 7. 2. Lightly grease a baking tray with 1 teaspoon of the oil and sprinkle with the rosemary. Season the chicken thighs on both sides and lay them flat over the rosemary to ensure even cooking. Arrange the onions, peppers, and zucchini around the edges of the chicken, season, and drizzle with the remaining oil. Cook for 20–25 minutes, until the chicken thighs are fully cooked, with no pink juices when pierced or an internal temperature of at least 74°C (165°F). 3. While the chicken is cooking, prepare the sauce. Test the spice level of the red chillies by tasting from the middle where the pith meets the seeds. Decide whether to use one or two chillies based on your preference. If neither are spicy enough, add a pinch of chilli flakes. Combine all sauce ingredients in a small food processor and blend, or finely chop and mix by hand. Pour into a jug and set aside. 4. Divide the cooked chicken and vegetables between 6 plates. Add a little watercress and a lemon wedge to each plate and serve with the sauce on the side.

Per Serving: Calories 489; Fat 24.38g; Sodium 421mg; Carbs 13.3g; Fiber 4.8g; Sugar 6.84g; Protein 53.19g

Easy Chicken Shawarma

Prep Time: 15 minutes | Cook Time: 15 minutes | Serves: 4-6

2 pounds boneless and skinless chicken

½ cup lemon juice

½ cup extra-virgin olive oil

3 tablespoons minced garlic

1½ teaspoons salt

½ teaspoon freshly ground black pepper

½ teaspoon ground cardamom

½ teaspoon cinnamon

1. Cut the chicken into ¼-inch strips and put them into a large bowl. 2. In a separate bowl, whisk together the lemon juice, garlic, salt, olive oil, pepper, cardamom, and cinnamon. 3. Add the dressing to the chicken and stir to coat all of the chicken. 4. Let the chicken sit for about 10 minutes. 5. In a large pan over medium-high heat, cook the chicken pieces for 12 minutes, using tongs to turn the chicken over every few minutes. 6. Serve.

Per Serving: Calories 424; Fat 26.46g; Sodium 781mg; Carbs 3.87g; Fiber 0.4g; Sugar 0.67g; Protein 41.29g

Chicken Piccata with Mushrooms and Zoodles

Prep Time: 25 minutes | Cook Time: 25 minutes | Serves: 4

1 pound thinly sliced chicken breasts

1½ teaspoons salt, divided

½ teaspoon freshly ground black pepper

¼ cup ground flaxseed

2 tablespoons almond flour

8 tablespoons extra-virgin olive oil, divided

4 tablespoons butter, divided

2 cups sliced mushrooms

½ cup chicken stock

¼ cup freshly squeezed lemon juice

¼ cup roughly chopped capers

Zucchini noodles, for serving

¼ cup chopped fresh flat-leaf Italian parsley, for garnish

1. Season the chicken with 1 teaspoon salt and the pepper. On a plate, combine the ground flaxseed and almond flour and dredge each chicken breast in the mixture. Set aside. 2. In a large skillet, heat 4 tablespoons olive oil and 1 tablespoon butter over medium-high heat. Working in batches if necessary, brown the chicken, 3 to 4 minutes per side. Remove from the skillet and keep warm. 3. Add the remaining 4 tablespoons olive oil and 1 tablespoon butter to the skillet along with mushrooms and sauté over medium heat until just tender, 6 to 8 minutes. 4. Add the chicken stock, capers, lemon juice, and remaining ½ teaspoon salt to the skillet and bring to a boil, whisking to incorporate any little browned bits that have stuck to the bottom of the skillet. Reduce the heat to low and whisk in the final 2 tablespoons butter. 5. Return the browned chicken to skillet, cover, and simmer over low heat until the chicken is cooked through and the sauce has thickened, 5 to 6 more minutes. 6. Serve the chicken and mushrooms warm over zucchini noodles, spooning the mushroom sauce over top and garnishing with the chopped parsley.

Per Serving: Calories 571; Fat 46.64g; Sodium 1181mg; Carbs 9.85g; Fiber 4.1g; Sugar 1.81g; Protein 30.29g

Grilled Chicken Shish Tawook

Prep Time: 15 minutes | Cook Time: 15 minutes | Serves: 4-6

2 tablespoons garlic, minced

2 tablespoons tomato paste

1 teaspoon smoked paprika

½ cup lemon juice

½ cup extra-virgin olive oil

1½ teaspoons salt

½ teaspoon freshly ground black pepper

2 pounds boneless and skinless chicken (breasts or thighs)

Rice, tzatziki, or hummus, for serving (optional)

1. In a large bowl, add the garlic, paprika, lemon juice, olive oil, salt, tomato paste, and pepper and whisk to combine. 2. Cut the chicken into ½-inch cubes and put them into the bowl; toss to coat with the marinade. Set aside for at least 10 minutes. 3. To grill, preheat the grill on high. Thread the chicken onto skewers and cook for 3 minutes per side, for a total of 9 minutes. 4. To cook in a pan, preheat the pan on high heat, add the chicken, and cook for 9 minutes, turning over the chicken using tongs. 5. Serve the chicken with rice, tzatziki, or hummus, if desired.

Per Serving: Calories 406; Fat 24.73g; Sodium 796mg; Carbs 4.42g; Fiber 0.6g; Sugar 1.48g; Protein 40.95g

Orange Chicken Baked in Foil with Fennel and Carrots

Prep Time: 10 minutes | Cook Time: 25 minutes | Serves: 4

2 oranges

2 tablespoons extra-virgin olive oil

1 shallot, sliced thin

1 teaspoon minced fresh tarragon

Salt and pepper

2 carrots, peeled and cut into 2-inch-long matchsticks

1 fennel bulb, stalks discarded, bulb halved, cored, and sliced thin

4 (6-ounce) boneless, skinless chicken breasts, trimmed of all visible fat

2 scallions, sliced thin

1. Adjust the oven rack to middle position and heat the oven to 450 degrees. Cut eight 12-inch square sheets of aluminum foil. 2. Cut away peel and pith from oranges. Quarter the oranges, then slice crosswise into ½-inch-thick pieces; transfer to a bowl. Combine the oil, shallot, tarragon, ¼ teaspoon salt, and ⅛ teaspoon pepper in a separate medium bowl. Toss the oranges with half of oil mixture. Add the carrots and fennel to the remaining oil mixture and toss to coat. Pound the chicken breasts to uniform thickness as needed. Pat breasts dry with paper towels and sprinkle with ¼ teaspoon salt and ⅛ teaspoon pepper. 3. Arrange the carrot-fennel mixture evenly in center of four pieces of foil. Lay the breasts over vegetables then spoon the orange mixture over top. 4. Place the remaining pieces of foil on top and fold edges over several times to seal. Place the packets on rimmed baking sheet and bake until chicken registers 160 degrees, about 25 minutes. (To test doneness of chicken, you will need to open one packet.) 5. Carefully open the packets, ensuring the steam escapes away from you, and let cool briefly. Smooth out the edges of foil and, using a spatula, gently slide the chicken, vegetables, and any accumulated juices onto individual plates. Sprinkle with the scallions and serve.

Per Serving: Calories 300; Fat 9.84g; Sodium 140mg; Carbs 12.9g; Fiber 3.1g; Sugar 7.73g; Protein 39.34g

Grilled Chicken Kebabs with Zucchini and Olives

Prep Time: 10 minutes | Cook Time: 20 minutes | Serves: 4

Nonstick cooking spray

¼ cup extra-virgin olive oil

2 tablespoons balsamic vinegar

1 teaspoon dried oregano, crushed between your fingers

1 pound boneless, skinless chicken breasts, cut into 1½-inch

pieces

2 medium zucchini, cut into 1-inch pieces (about 2½ cups)

½ cup Kalamata olives, pitted and halved

2 tablespoons olive brine

¼ cup torn fresh basil leaves

1. Coat the cold grill with nonstick cooking spray. Heat the grill to medium-high. 2. In a small bowl, whisk together the oil, vinegar, and oregano. Divide the marinade between two large plastic zip-top bags. 3. Add the chicken to one bag and the zucchini to another. Seal and massage the marinade into both the chicken and zucchini. 4. Thread the chicken onto 6 (12-inch) wooden skewers. Thread the zucchini onto 8 or 9 (12-inch) wooden skewers. Cook the kebabs in batches on the grill for 5 minutes, flip, and grill for 5 minutes more, until any chicken juices run clear. 5. Remove the chicken and zucchini from the skewers and put in a large serving bowl. Toss with the olives, olive brine, and basil and serve.

Per Serving: Calories 295; Fat 17.68g; Sodium 187mg; Carbs 6.17g; Fiber 1.9g; Sugar 1.21g; Protein 28.5g

One-Pan Parsley Chicken Thighs and Potatoes

Prep Time: 5 minutes | Cook Time: 25 minutes | Serves: 6

1½ pounds boneless, skinless chicken thighs, cut into 1-inch cubes

1 tablespoon extra-virgin olive oil

1½ pounds Yukon Gold potatoes, unpeeled, cut into ½-inch cubes (about 6 small potatoes)

2 garlic cloves, minced (about 1 teaspoon)

¼ cup apple cider vinegar

1 cup low-sodium or no-salt-added chicken broth

1 tablespoon Dijon mustard

¼ teaspoon kosher or sea salt

¼ teaspoon freshly ground black pepper

1 cup chopped fresh flat-leaf (Italian) parsley, including stems

1 tablespoon freshly squeezed lemon juice (½ small lemon)

1. Pat the chicken dry with a few paper towels. In a large skillet over medium-high heat, heat the oil. Add the chicken and cook for 5 minutes, stirring only after the chicken has browned on one side. Remove the chicken from the pan with a slotted spoon, and put it on a plate; it will not yet be fully cooked. Leave the skillet on the stove. 2. Add the potatoes to the skillet and cook for 5 minutes, stirring only after the potatoes have become golden and crispy on one side. Push the potatoes to the side of the skillet, add the garlic, and cook, stirring constantly, for 1 minute. Add the apple cider vinegar and cook for 1 minute, until nearly evaporated. Add the chicken broth, mustard, salt, pepper, and reserved chicken pieces. Turn the heat up to high, and bring to a boil. 3. Once boiling, cover the skillet, reduce the heat to medium-low, and cook for 10 to 12 minutes, until the potatoes are tender and the internal temperature of the chicken measures 165°F on a meat thermometer and any juices run clear. 4. During the last minute of cooking, stir in the parsley. Remove from the heat, stir in the lemon juice, and serve.

Per Serving: Calories 251; Fat 6.97g; Sodium 328mg; Carbs 22.81g; Fiber 3g; Sugar 2.11g; Protein 25.25g

Chicken Provençal

Prep Time: 10 minutes | Cook Time: 8 hours | Serves: 4

4 (6-ounce) boneless, skinless chicken breast halves

2 teaspoons dried basil

1 teaspoon dried oregano

½ teaspoon sea salt

¼ teaspoon black pepper

1 yellow bell pepper, diced

2 cloves garlic, minced

One 15-ounce can cannellini beans, rinsed and drained

One 15-ounce can diced tomatoes, with the juice

4 basil sprigs, for garnish

1. Place the chicken in the slow cooker. Sprinkle with the basil, salt, oregano, and black pepper. Add the bell pepper, cannellini beans, garlic, and tomatoes. 2. Cover and cook on low for 8 hours until the chicken is cooked thoroughly. 3. Serve hot, garnished with a basil sprig.

Per Serving: Calories 339; Fat 6.95g; Sodium 1449mg; Carbs 29.39g; Fiber 8.2g; Sugar 3.05g; Protein 57.31g

Oven Roasted Chicken Breasts with Root Vegetables

Prep Time: 10 minutes | Cook Time: 25-35 minutes | Serves: 4

12 ounces Brussels sprouts, trimmed and halved

12 ounces red potatoes, unpeeled, cut into 1-inch pieces

8 ounces parsnips, peeled and cut into 2-inch lengths, thick ends halved lengthwise

4 carrots, peeled and cut into 2-inch lengths, thick ends halved lengthwise

4 shallots, peeled and halved lengthwise

6 garlic cloves, peeled

3 tablespoons extra-virgin olive oil

4 teaspoons minced fresh thyme or 1½ teaspoons dried

2 teaspoons minced fresh rosemary or ¾ teaspoon dried

Salt and pepper

2 (12-ounce) bone-in split chicken breasts, trimmed of all visible fat and halved crosswise

Lemon wedges

1. Adjust the oven rack to upper-middle position and heat the oven to 475 degrees. Combine the Brussels sprouts, potatoes, shallots, parsnips, carrots, garlic, 2 tablespoons oil, 2 teaspoons thyme, ¼ teaspoon salt, 1 teaspoon rosemary, and ¼ teaspoon pepper in a bowl. Combine the remaining 1 tablespoon oil, remaining 1 teaspoon rosemary, ¼ teaspoon salt, remaining 2 teaspoons thyme, and ⅛ teaspoon pepper in a separate bowl. 2. Pound the chicken breast pieces to uniform thickness as needed, then pat dry with paper towels. Using your fingers, gently loosen the skin covering each breast piece, then rub the oil mixture evenly under skin. 3. Spread the vegetables cut side down in single layer over three-quarters of rimmed baking sheet. Place the chicken pieces skin side up on empty portion of sheet. Roast until the vegetables are browned and tender and the chicken registers 160 degrees, 25 to 35 minutes, rotating the sheet halfway through roasting. Discard the chicken skin. Toss the vegetables with any accumulated chicken juices. Serve with the lemon wedges.

Per Serving: Calories 457; Fat 13.69g; Sodium 464mg; Carbs 41.63g; Fiber 9.9g; Sugar 9.72g; Protein 44.16g

Greek Yogurt Marinated Chicken

Prep Time: 15 minutes | Cook Time: 30 minutes | Serves: 2

½ cup plain Greek yogurt
3 garlic cloves, minced
2 tablespoons minced fresh oregano (or 1 tablespoon dried oregano)

Zest of 1 lemon
1 tablespoon olive oil
½ teaspoon salt
2 (4-ounce) boneless, skinless chicken breasts

1. In a medium bowl, add the yogurt, garlic, lemon zest, olive oil, oregano, and salt and stir to combine. If the yogurt is very thick, you may need to add a few tablespoons of water or a squeeze of lemon juice to thin it a bit. 2. Add the chicken to the bowl and toss it in the marinade to coat it well. Cover and refrigerate the chicken for at least 30 minutes or up to overnight. 3. Preheat the oven to 350°F and set the rack to the middle position. 4. Place the chicken in a baking dish and roast for 30 minutes, or until chicken reaches an internal temperature of 165°F.

Per Serving: Calories 216; Fat 8.84g; Sodium 651mg; Carbs 4.91g; Fiber 0.6g; Sugar 1.66g; Protein 28.69g

Roasted Chicken with Butternut Squash and Kale

Prep Time: 10 minutes | Cook Time: 25-35 minutes | Serves: 4

5 tablespoons extra-virgin olive oil
2 tablespoons minced fresh sage
Salt and pepper
¾ cup plain low-fat yogurt
1 tablespoon water
7 garlic cloves, peeled (6 halved, 1 minced)
1 teaspoon grated orange zest
2 pounds butternut squash, peeled, seeded, and cut into 1-inch

pieces (6 cups)
8 shallots, peeled and halved lengthwise
2 teaspoons paprika
2 (12-ounce) bone-in split chicken breasts, trimmed of all visible fat and halved crosswise
8 ounces kale, stemmed and cut into 2-inch pieces
½ cup unsweetened dried cherries

1. Adjust the oven rack to upper-middle position and heat the oven to 475 degrees. Combine the oil, ½ teaspoon salt, sage, and ½ teaspoon pepper in a bowl. Combine the yogurt, water, orange zest, minced garlic, and 1 tablespoon oil mixture in a separate bowl. Season with the pepper to taste and refrigerate sauce until ready to serve. 2. Combine the squash, halved garlic cloves, shallots, and 3 tablespoons oil mixture in a large bowl; set aside. Stir the paprika into the remaining oil mixture. Pound the chicken breast pieces to uniform thickness as needed, then pat dry with paper towels. Using your fingers, gently loosen the skin covering each breast piece, then rub the remaining oil mixture evenly under skin. 3. Spread the vegetable mixture in single layer over three-quarters of rimmed baking sheet. Place the chicken pieces skin side up on empty portion of sheet and roast for 15 minutes. 4. Meanwhile, vigorously squeeze and massage the kale with hands in a now-empty bowl until leaves are uniformly darkened and slightly wilted, about 1 minute. Rotate the sheet, stir the kale and cherries into the vegetables, and roast until the vegetables are browned and tender and the chicken registers 160 degrees, 10 to 20 minutes, stirring the vegetables halfway through roasting. 5. Discard the chicken skin. Toss the vegetables with any accumulated chicken juices. Serve, passing yogurt sauce separately.

Per Serving: Calories 467; Fat 21.58g; Sodium 152mg; Carbs 24.8g; Fiber 6.3g; Sugar 13.58g; Protein 46.66g

Roasted Chicken with Cauliflower and Tomatoes

Prep Time: 10 minutes | Cook Time: 25-35 minutes | Serves: 4

1 head cauliflower (2 pounds), cored and cut into 8 wedges through stem end

6 shallots, peeled and halved lengthwise

¼ cup extra-virgin olive oil

2 tablespoons chopped fresh sage or 2 teaspoons dried

Salt and pepper

2 garlic cloves, minced

1 teaspoon grated lemon zest, plus lemon wedges for serving

2 (12-ounce) bone-in split chicken breasts, trimmed of all visible fat and halved crosswise

8 ounces grape tomatoes

1 tablespoon chopped fresh parsley

1. Adjust the oven rack to upper-middle position and heat the oven to 475 degrees. Combine the cauliflower, shallots, 2 tablespoons oil, 1 tablespoon sage, ¼ teaspoon salt, and ½ teaspoon pepper in a bowl. Combine the garlic, lemon zest, remaining 2 tablespoons oil, remaining 1 tablespoon sage, ¼ teaspoon salt, and ⅛ teaspoon pepper in a separate bowl. 2. Pound the chicken breast pieces to uniform thickness as needed, then pat dry with paper towels. Using your fingers, gently loosen the skin covering each breast piece, then rub the oil mixture evenly under skin. 3. Spread the vegetables cut side down in single layer over three-quarters of rimmed baking sheet. Place the chicken pieces skin side up on empty portion of sheet and roast for 15 minutes. Rotate the sheet, spread the tomatoes over vegetables, and roast until the vegetables are browned and tender and the chicken registers 160 degrees, 10 to 20 minutes. Discard the chicken skin. Toss the vegetables with parsley and any accumulated chicken juices. Serve with the lemon wedges.

Per Serving: Calories 390; Fat 17.13g; Sodium 161mg; Carbs 17.79g; Fiber 6g; Sugar 7.34g; Protein 43.22g

Lemony Chicken with Potatoes and Olives

Prep Time: 20 minutes | Cook Time: 21 minutes | Serves: 4

4 (5- to 7-ounce) bone-in chicken thighs, trimmed

½ teaspoon table salt

¼ teaspoon pepper

2 teaspoons extra-virgin olive oil, plus extra for drizzling

4 garlic cloves, peeled and smashed

½ cup chicken broth

1 small lemon, sliced thin

1½ pounds fingerling potatoes, unpeeled

¼ cup pitted brine-cured green or black olives, halved

2 tablespoons coarsely chopped fresh parsley

1. Pat the chicken dry with paper towels and sprinkle with the salt and pepper. Using the highest sauté function, heat the oil in the instant pot for 5 minutes (or until just smoking). Place the chicken skin side down in the pot and cook until well browned on first side, about 5 minutes; transfer to plate. 2. Add the garlic to fat left in the pot and cook, Using the highest sauté function, until golden and fragrant, about 2 minutes. Stir in the broth and lemon, scraping up any browned bits. Return the chicken skin side up to the pot and add any accumulated juices. Arrange the potatoes on top. Lock the lid in place and close the pressure release valve. Set to the high pressure cook function and cook for 9 minutes. 3. Turn off the instant pot and quickly release pressure. Carefully remove the lid, ensuring the steam escapes away from you. Transfer chicken to a serving dish and discard skin, if desired. Stir the olives and parsley into potatoes and season with the salt and pepper to taste. Serve the chicken with potatoes.

Per Serving: Calories 377; Fat 10.44g; Sodium 642mg; Carbs 32.59g; Fiber 4.2g; Sugar 1.95g; Protein 37.49g

Bake Lemon Chicken Thighs Foil Packets

Prep Time: 5 minutes | Cook Time: 22 minutes | Serves: 4

4 bone-in chicken thighs, skin and fat removed

2 tablespoons olive oil

1 teaspoon garlic powder

1 teaspoon salt

Black pepper

1 lemon, sliced

1. Preheat the air fryer to 380°F. 2. Coat the chicken thighs in the olive oil, garlic powder, and salt. 3. Tear off four pieces of aluminum foil, with each sheet being large enough to envelop one chicken thigh. 4. Place one chicken thigh onto each piece of foil, season it with the black pepper, and then top it with slices of lemon. 5. Bake for 20 to 22 minutes, or until the internal temperature of the chicken has reached 165°F. 6. Remove the foil packets from the air fryer. Carefully open each packet to avoid a steam burn. Serve.

Per Serving: Calories 229; Fat 12.26g; Sodium 813mg; Carbs 1.76g; Fiber 0.3g; Sugar 0.32g; Protein 28.51g

Chicken Baked in Foil with Zucchini and Tomatoes

Prep Time: 10 minutes | Cook Time: 25 minutes | Serves: 4

2 zucchini, sliced ¼ inch thick

Salt and pepper

2 tablespoons extra-virgin olive oil

2 garlic cloves, minced

1 teaspoon minced fresh oregano or ¼ teaspoon dried

⅛ teaspoon red pepper flakes

3 plum tomatoes, cored, seeded, and cut into ½-inch pieces

4 (6-ounce) boneless, skinless chicken breasts, trimmed of all visible fat

¼ cup chopped fresh basil

Lemon wedges

1. Toss the zucchini with ¼ teaspoon salt in a colander and let drain for 30 minutes. Spread the zucchini out on several layers of paper towels and pat dry; transfer to a bowl. Adjust the oven rack to middle position and heat the oven to 450 degrees. Cut eight 12-inch square sheets of aluminum foil. 2. Combine the oil, oregano, garlic, pepper flakes, and ⅛ teaspoon pepper in a medium bowl. Toss the zucchini with half of oil mixture in a separate bowl. Add the tomatoes to the remaining oil mixture and toss to coat. Pound the chicken breasts to uniform thickness as needed. Pat the breasts dry with paper towels and sprinkle with ¼ teaspoon salt and ⅛ teaspoon pepper. 3. Arrange the zucchini evenly in center of four pieces of foil. Lay the breasts over zucchini, then spoon the tomato mixture over top. 4. Place the remaining pieces of foil on top and fold edges over several times to seal. Place the packets on the rimmed baking sheet and bake until the chicken registers 160 degrees, about 25 minutes. (To test doneness of chicken, you will need to open one packet.) 5. Carefully open the packets, ensuring the steam escapes away from you, and let cool briefly. Smooth out the edges of foil and, using a spatula, gently slide the chicken, vegetables, and any accumulated juices onto individual plates. Sprinkle with the basil and serve with the lemon wedges.

Per Serving: Calories 277; Fat 10g; Sodium 388mg; Carbs 6.53g; Fiber 1.8g; Sugar 4.01g; Protein 39.59g

Whole Roast Chicken with Potatoes

Prep Time: 15 minutes | Cook Time: 4-5 hours | Serves: 4

4 to 6 Yukon gold potatoes, quartered
1 whole skinless chicken, 4 to 5 pounds
1 large yellow onion, quartered
4 or 5 cloves garlic, whole
2 teaspoons sea salt
1 teaspoon paprika
1 teaspoon onion powder

½ teaspoon dried thyme
1 teaspoon dried oregano
1 teaspoon dried rosemary
½ teaspoon dried parsley
½ teaspoon cayenne pepper
½ teaspoon black pepper

1. Place the potatoes in the slow cooker. 2. Clean out the chicken cavity. Rinse the chicken, inside and out. Pat dry. 3. Stuff the cavity with the onion and garlic. 4. In a small bowl, combine the salt, paprika, thyme, oregano, cayenne pepper, rosemary, onion powder, parsley, and black pepper. Rub the mixture all over the chicken. 5. Place the chicken over the potatoes in the slow cooker, breast-side down. 6. Cook on high for 4 to 5 hours, or on low for 8 hours. 7. When serving, spoon up some of the juice on the bottom of the slow cooker and ladle over the chicken.

Per Serving: Calories 455; Fat 6.84g; Sodium 1358mg; Carbs 43.1g; Fiber 6g; Sugar 3.42g; Protein 53.64g

Chicken with Spiced Freekeh and Preserved Lemon

Prep Time: 20 minutes | Cook Time: 11 minutes | Serves: 4

2 tablespoons extra-virgin olive oil, plus extra for drizzling
1 onion, chopped fine
4 garlic cloves, minced
1½ teaspoons smoked paprika
¼ teaspoon ground cardamom
¼ teaspoon red pepper flakes
2¼ cups chicken broth
1½ cups cracked freekeh, rinsed

2 (12-ounce) bone-in split chicken breasts, halved crosswise and trimmed
½ teaspoon table salt
¼ teaspoon pepper
¼ cup chopped fresh cilantro
2 tablespoons sesame seeds, toasted
½ preserved lemon, pulp and white pith removed, rind rinsed and minced (2 tablespoons)

1. Using the highest sauté function, heat the oil in the instant pot until shimmering. Add the onion and cook until softened, about 5 minutes. Stir in the garlic, paprika, cardamom, and pepper flakes and cook until fragrant, about 30 seconds. Stir in the broth and freekeh. Sprinkle the chicken with salt and pepper. Nestle the skin side up into freekeh mixture. Lock the lid in place and close the pressure release valve. Set to the high pressure cook function and cook for 5 minutes. 2. Turn off the instant pot and quickly release pressure. Carefully remove the lid, ensuring the steam escapes away from you. Transfer the chicken to serving dish and discard the skin, if desired. Tent with aluminum foil and allow to rest while finishing freekeh. 3. Gently fluff the freekeh with a fork. Lay clean dish towel over pot, replace the lid, and let sit for 5 minutes. Season with the salt and pepper to taste. Transfer the freekeh to a serving dish with the chicken and sprinkle with the cilantro, sesame seeds, and preserved lemon. Drizzle the with extra oil and serve.

Per Serving: Calories 572; Fat 16.27g; Sodium 1377mg; Carbs 53.47g; Fiber 11.1g; Sugar 2.73g; Protein 56.14g

Moroccan Chicken with Apricots and Olives

Prep Time: 10 minutes | Cook Time: 2 hours | Serves: 4

3 pounds skinless chicken thighs

1 yellow onion, cut into ½-inch wedges

1 teaspoon ground cumin

½ teaspoon ground ginger

½ teaspoon ground coriander

¼ teaspoon ground cinnamon·

¼ teaspoon cayenne pepper

Sea salt

Black pepper

1 bay leaf

⅓ cup chicken stock

One 15-ounce can chickpeas, drained and rinsed

½ cup green olives

½ cup dried Turkish apricots

⅓ cup sliced almonds, toasted

1. In a large bowl, mix the chicken thighs and the onion. Add the cumin, cinnamon, coriander, ginger, and cayenne and toss to coat. Season the spiced chicken and onion with the salt and pepper. 2. Place the chicken and onion into the slow cooker. Add the bay leaf and pour in chicken stock. 3. Cover and cook on high for 2 hours. 4. Stir in the chickpeas, olives, and apricots. Cover and cook until the chicken is tender and fully cooked and the apricots are plump, about 1 hour more. 5. Remove the bay leaf and season the juices with salt and pepper. 6. Meanwhile, preheat the oven to 350°F. Place the almonds in a pie plate and toast for about 7 minutes, until fragrant and lightly golden. Watch them so they don't burn. 7. Spoon the hot chicken, vegetables, and juices into the shallow bowls, sprinkle with the toasted almonds, and serve.

Per Serving: Calories 625; Fat 12.55g; Sodium 1018mg; Carbs 40.5g; Fiber 9.7g; Sugar 14.79g; Protein 86.18g

Tahini Chicken and Rice Bowls

Prep Time: 10 minutes | Cook Time: 15 minutes | Serves: 4

1 cup uncooked instant brown rice

¼ cup tahini or peanut butter (tahini for nut-free)

¼ cup 2% plain Greek yogurt

2 tablespoons chopped scallions, green and white parts (2 scallions)

1 tablespoon freshly squeezed lemon juice (from ½ medium lemon)

1 tablespoon water

1 teaspoon ground cumin

¾ teaspoon ground cinnamon

¼ teaspoon kosher or sea salt

2 cups chopped cooked chicken breast (about 1 pound)

½ cup chopped dried apricots

2 cups peeled and chopped seedless cucumber (1 large cucumber)

4 teaspoons sesame seeds

Fresh mint leaves, for serving (optional)

1. Cook the brown rice according to the package instructions. 2. While the rice is cooking, in a medium bowl, mix together the tahini, yogurt, water, cumin, cinnamon, scallions, lemon juice, and salt. Transfer half the tahini mixture to another medium bowl. Mix the chicken into the first bowl. 3. When the rice is done, mix it into the second bowl of tahini (the one without the chicken). 4. To assemble, divide the chicken among four bowls. Spoon the rice mixture next to the chicken in each bowl. Next to the chicken, place the dried apricots, and in the remaining empty section, add the cucumbers. Sprinkle with the sesame seeds, and top with the mint, if desired, and serve.

Per Serving: Calories 454; Fat 11.89g; Sodium 305mg; Carbs 55.77g; Fiber 4.9g; Sugar 12.02g; Protein 32.34g

Spiced Chicken Kebab

Prep Time: 35 minutes | Cook Time: 25 minutes | Serves: 4

¼ cup olive oil

1 teaspoon garlic powder

1 teaspoon onion powder

1 teaspoon ground cumin

½ teaspoon dried oregano

½ teaspoon dried basil

¼ cup lemon juice

1 tablespoon apple cider vinegar

Olive oil cooking spray

1 pound boneless skinless chicken thighs, cut into 1-inch pieces

1 red bell pepper, cut into 1-inch pieces

1 red onion, cut into 1-inch pieces

1 zucchini, cut into 1-inch pieces

12 cherry tomatoes

1. In a large bowl, mix together the olive oil, onion powder, cumin, garlic powder, oregano, basil, lemon juice, and apple cider vinegar. 2. Spray six skewers with olive oil cooking spray. 3. On each skewer, slide on a piece of chicken, then a piece of bell pepper, onion, zucchini, and finally a tomato and then repeat. Each skewer should have at least two pieces of each item. 4. Once all of the skewers are prepared, place them in a 9-by-13-inch baking dish and pour the olive oil marinade over the top of the skewers. Turn each skewer so that all sides of the chicken and vegetables are coated. 5. Cover the dish with plastic wrap and place it in the refrigerator for 30 minutes. 6. After 30 minutes, preheat the air fryer to 380°F. (If using a grill attachment, make sure it is inside the air fryer during preheating.) 7. Remove the skewers from the marinade and lay them in a single layer in the air fryer basket. If the air fryer has a grill attachment, you can also lay them on this instead. 8. Cook for 10 minutes. Rotate the kebabs, then cook them for 15 minutes more. 9. Remove the skewers from the air fryer and let them rest for 5 minutes before serving.

Per Serving: Calories 288; Fat 15.92g; Sodium 69mg; Carbs 9.57g; Fiber 2.1g; Sugar 4.8g; Protein 27.1g

Chapter 6 Beef, Pork, and Lamb Recipes

Grilled Greek Beef Kebabs

Prep Time: 10 minutes | Cook Time: 10 minutes | Serves: 6

¼ cup olive oil

Juice of 1 lemon

1 tablespoon dried oregano

2 cloves garlic, minced

5 bay leaves

Sea salt and freshly ground pepper, to taste

2 pounds beef sirloin, cut into 2-inch cubes

1. Combine all the ingredients except the meat in a plastic bag. Add the meat and shake to coat. 2. Marinate for up to 24 hours and drain. 3. Skewer the meat onto 8-inch skewers and grill on medium heat for 8–10 minutes, turning the skewers halfway through the cooking time.

Per Serving: Calories 290; Fat 16.08g; Sodium 474mg; Carbs 1.71g; Fiber 0.4g; Sugar 0.23g; Protein 33.32g

Meatballs in Creamy Almond Sauce

Prep Time: 15 minutes | Cook Time: 35 minutes | Serves: 4-6

8 ounces ground veal or pork

8 ounces ground beef

½ cup finely minced onion, divided

1 large egg, beaten

¼ cup almond flour

1½ teaspoons salt, divided

1 teaspoon garlic powder

¼ cup unsweetened almond butter

½ teaspoon freshly ground black pepper

½ teaspoon ground nutmeg

2 teaspoons chopped fresh flat-leaf Italian parsley, plus ¼ cup, divided

½ cup extra-virgin olive oil, divided

¼ cup slivered almonds

1 cup chicken broth

1. In a large bowl, combine the veal, beef, ¼ cup onion, and the egg and mix well with a fork. In a small bowl, whisk together the almond flour, garlic powder, pepper, 1 teaspoon salt, and nutmeg. Add to the meat mixture along with 2 teaspoons chopped parsley and incorporate well. Form the mixture into small meatballs, about 1 inch in diameter, and place on a plate. Let sit for 10 minutes at room temperature. 2. In a large skillet, heat ¼ cup oil over medium-high heat. Add the meatballs to the hot oil and brown on all sides, cooking in batches if necessary, 2 to 3 minutes per side. Remove from skillet and keep warm. 3. In the hot skillet, sauté the remaining ¼ cup minced onion in the remaining ¼ cup olive oil for 5 minutes. Reduce the heat to medium-low and add the slivered almonds. Sauté until the almonds are golden, another 3 to 5 minutes. 4. In a small bowl, whisk together the chicken broth, almond butter, and remaining ½ teaspoon salt. Add to the skillet and bring to a boil, stirring constantly. Reduce the heat to low, return the meatballs to skillet, and cover. Cook until the meatballs are cooked through, another 8 to 10 minutes. 5. Remove from the heat, stir in the remaining ¼ cup chopped parsley, and serve the meatballs warm and drizzled with the almond sauce.

Per Serving: Calories 542; Fat 43.58g; Sodium 886mg; Carbs 11.29g; Fiber 2.9g; Sugar 2.33g; Protein 27.66g

Savory Italian Pot Roast

Prep Time: 15 minutes | Cook Time: 6 hours | Serves: 8

One 3-pound beef chuck roast, trimmed and halved crosswise

4 cloves garlic, halved lengthwise

1½ teaspoons coarse sea salt

1 teaspoon black pepper

1 tablespoon olive oil

1 large yellow onion, cut into 8 wedges

1¼ pounds small white potatoes

One 28-ounce can whole tomatoes in purée

1 tablespoon chopped fresh rosemary leaves (or 1 teaspoon dried and crumbled rosemary)

1. With a sharp paring knife, cut four slits in each of the beef roast halves, and stuff the slits with one-half of the garlic halves. Generously season the beef with the salt and pepper. 2. In a large skillet, heat the olive oil over medium-high heat, swirling to coat the bottom of the pan. Cook the beef until browned on all sides, about 5 minutes. 3. Combine the beef, onion, potatoes, rosemary, tomatoes, and the remaining garlic in the slow cooker. 4. Cover and cook until the meat is fork-tender, on high for about 6 hours. 5. Transfer the meat to a cutting board. Thinly slice, and discard any fat or gristle. 6. Skim the fat from the top of the sauce in the slow cooker. 7. Serve hot, dividing the beef and vegetables among the eight bowls, and generously spooning the sauce over the top.

Per Serving: Calories 316; Fat 11.78g; Sodium 618mg; Carbs 16.61g; Fiber 2.9g; Sugar 1.63g; Protein 37.41g

Flank Steak with Citrusy Herb Pistou

Prep Time: 10 minutes | Cook Time: 20 minutes | Serves: 4

1 pound flank steak

8 tablespoons extra-virgin olive oil, divided

2 teaspoons salt, divided

1 teaspoon freshly ground black pepper, divided

½ cup chopped fresh flat-leaf Italian parsley

¼ cup chopped fresh mint leaves

2 garlic cloves, roughly chopped

Zest and juice of 1 orange or 2 clementines

1 teaspoon red pepper flakes (optional)

1 tablespoon red wine vinegar

1. Heat the grill to medium-high heat or, if using an oven, preheat to 400°F. 2. Rub the steak with 2 tablespoons olive oil and sprinkle with 1 teaspoon salt and ½ teaspoon pepper. Let sit at room temperature while you make the pistou. 3. In a food processor, combine the parsley, orange zest and juice, remaining 1 teaspoon salt, mint, garlic, red pepper flakes (if using), and remaining ½ teaspoon pepper. Pulse until finely chopped. With the processor running, stream in the red wine vinegar and remaining 6 tablespoons olive oil until well combined. This pistou will be more oil-based than traditional basil pesto. 4. Cook the steak on the grill, 6 to 8 minutes per side. Remove from the grill and allow to rest for 10 minutes on a cutting board. If cooking in the oven, heat a large oven-safe skillet (cast iron works great) over high heat. Add the steak and sear, 1 to 2 minutes per side, until browned. Transfer the skillet to the oven and cook 10 to 12 minutes, or until the steak reaches your desired temperature. 5. To serve, slice the steak and drizzle with the pistou.

Per Serving: Calories 428; Fat 34.36g; Sodium 1234mg; Carbs 4.45g; Fiber 0.9g; Sugar 1.93g; Protein 25.3g

Balsamic Pork Chops with Peppers and Onions

Prep Time: 5 minutes | Cook Time: 25 minutes | Serves: 4

4 (4-ounce) pork chops, untrimmed

1½ teaspoons salt, divided

1 teaspoon freshly ground black pepper, divided

½ cup extra-virgin olive oil, divided

1 red or orange bell pepper, thinly sliced

1 green bell pepper, thinly sliced

1 small yellow onion, thinly sliced

2 teaspoons dried Italian herbs (such as oregano, parsley, or rosemary)

2 garlic cloves, minced

1 tablespoon balsamic vinegar

1. Season the pork chops with 1 teaspoon salt and ½ teaspoon pepper. 2. In a large skillet, heat ¼ cup olive oil over medium-high heat. Fry the pork chops in the oil until browned and almost cooked through but not fully cooked, 4 to 5 minutes per side, depending on the thickness of chops. Remove from the skillet and cover to keep warm. 3. Pour the remaining ¼ cup olive oil in the skillet and sauté the sliced peppers, onions, and herbs over medium-high heat until tender, 6 to 8 minutes. Add the garlic, stirring to combine, and return the pork to skillet. Cover, reduce the heat to low, and cook for another 2 to 3 minutes, or until the pork is cooked through. 4. Turn off the heat. Using a slotted spoon, transfer the pork, peppers, and onions to a serving platter. Add the vinegar to the oil in the skillet and whisk to combine well. Drizzle the vinaigrette over the pork and serve warm.

Per Serving: Calories 414; Fat 31.39g; Sodium 942mg; Carbs 7.25g; Fiber 1.1g; Sugar 1.93g; Protein 26.01g

Moroccan Style Stuffed Peppers

Prep Time: 10 minutes | Cook Time: 30 minutes | Serves: 4

¼ cup, plus 2 tablespoons extra-virgin olive oil, divided

2 large red bell peppers

1 pound ground beef

1 small onion, finely chopped

2 garlic cloves, minced

2 tablespoons chopped fresh sage or 2 teaspoons dried sage

1 teaspoon salt

1 teaspoon ground allspice

½ teaspoon freshly ground black pepper

½ cup chopped fresh flat-leaf Italian parsley

½ cup chopped baby arugula leaves

½ cup chopped walnuts

1 tablespoon freshly squeezed orange juice

1. Preheat the oven to 425°F. 2. Drizzle 1 tablespoon olive oil in a rimmed baking sheet and swirl to coat the bottom. 3. Remove the stems from the peppers and cut in half lengthwise, then remove the seeds and membranes. Place cut-side down on the prepared baking sheet and roast until just softened, 5 to 8 minutes. Remove from the oven and let cool. 4. Meanwhile, in a large skillet, heat 1 tablespoon olive oil over medium-high heat. Add the beef and onions and sauté until the meat is browned and cooked through, 8 to 10 minutes. Add the garlic, salt, allspice, sage, and pepper and sauté for 2 more minutes. 5. Remove from the heat and cool slightly. Stir in the parsley, arugula, orange juice, walnuts, and remaining ¼ cup olive oil and mix well. 6. Stuff the filling into each pepper half. Return to the oven and cook for 5 minutes. Serve warm.

Per Serving: Calories 462; Fat 37.06g; Sodium 665mg; Carbs 7.98g; Fiber 2.3g; Sugar 2.73g; Protein 27.66g

Simple Pork Souvlaki

Prep Time: 1 hour 15 minutes | Cook Time: 10 minutes | Serves: 4

1 (1½-pound) pork loin

2 tablespoons garlic, minced

⅓ cup extra-virgin olive oil

⅓ cup lemon juice

1 tablespoon dried oregano

1 teaspoon salt

1. Cut the pork into 1-inch cubes and put them into a bowl or plastic zip-top bag. 2. In a large bowl, mix together the garlic, lemon juice, olive oil, oregano, and salt. 3. Pour the marinade over the pork and let it marinate for at least 1 hour. 4. Preheat a grill, grill pan, or lightly oiled skillet to high heat. Using wood or metal skewers, thread the pork onto the skewers. 5. Cook the skewers for 3 minutes on each side, for 12 minutes in total. 6. Serve.

Per Serving: Calories 394; Fat 24.82g; Sodium 666mg; Carbs 3.14g; Fiber 0.4g; Sugar 0.57g; Protein 38.47g

Braised Lamb Shanks with Bell Pepper and Harissa

Prep Time: 10 minutes | Cook Time: 1 hour 20 minutes | Serves: 4

4 (10- to 12-ounce) lamb shanks, trimmed

¾ teaspoon salt, divided

1 tablespoon extra-virgin olive oil

1 onion, chopped

1 red bell pepper, stemmed, seeded, and cut into 1-inch pieces

¼ cup harissa, divided

4 garlic cloves, minced

1 tablespoon tomato paste

½ cup chicken broth

1 bay leaf

2 tablespoons chopped fresh mint

1. Pat the lamb shanks dry with paper towels and sprinkle with ½ teaspoon salt. Using the highest sauté function, heat the oil in the instant pot for 5 minutes (or until just smoking). Brown 2 shanks on all sides, 8 to 10 minutes; transfer to a plate. Repeat with the remaining shanks; transfer to the plate. 2. Add the onion, bell pepper, and remaining ¼ teaspoon salt to fat left in the pot and cook, using the highest sauté function, until the vegetables are softened, about 5 minutes. Stir in 2 tablespoons harissa, garlic, and tomato paste and cook until fragrant, about 30 seconds. Stir in the broth and bay leaf, scraping up any browned bits. Nestle the shanks into the pot and add any accumulated juices. Lock the lid in place and close the pressure release valve. Set to the high pressure cook function and cook for 60 minutes. 3. Turn off the instant pot and let pressure release naturally for 15 minutes. Quick-release any remaining pressure, then carefully remove the lid, ensuring the steam escapes away from you. Transfer the shanks to a serving dish, tent with aluminum foil, and allow to rest while finishing sauce. 4. Strain the braising liquid through a fine-mesh strainer into fat separator. Discard the bay leaf and transfer the solids to a blender. Allow the braising liquid to settle for 5 minutes, then pour ¾ cup defatted liquid into the blender with solids; discard the remaining liquid. Add the remaining 2 tablespoons harissa and process until smooth, about 1 minute. Season with the salt and pepper to taste. Pour portion of sauce over shanks and sprinkle with the mint. Serve, passing the remaining sauce separately.

Per Serving: Calories 402; Fat 14.26g; Sodium 789mg; Carbs 5.68g; Fiber 1g; Sugar 2.41g; Protein 63.63g

Grilled Beef Kefta

Prep Time: 10 minutes | Cook Time: 5 minutes | Serves: 4

1 medium onion

⅓ cup fresh Italian parsley

1 pound ground beef

¼ teaspoon ground cumin

¼ teaspoon cinnamon

1 teaspoon salt

½ teaspoon freshly ground black pepper

1. Preheat a grill or grill pan to high. 2. Mince the onion and parsley in a food processor until finely chopped. 3. In a large bowl, using your hands, combine the beef with the onion mix, ground cumin, cinnamon, salt, and pepper. 4. Divide the meat into 6 portions. Form each portion into a flat oval. 5. Place the patties on the grill or grill pan and cook for 3 minutes on each side. 6. Serve.

Per Serving: Calories 163; Fat 5.78g; Sodium 660mg; Carbs 3.27g; Fiber 0.8g; Sugar 1.22g; Protein 24.79g

Homemade Beef Sliders with Pepper Slaw

Prep Time: 10 minutes | Cook Time: 10 minutes | Serves: 4

Nonstick cooking spray

1 (8-ounce) package white button mushrooms

2 tablespoons extra-virgin olive oil, divided

1 pound ground beef (93% lean)

2 garlic cloves, minced (about 1 teaspoon)

½ teaspoon kosher or sea salt, divided

¼ teaspoon freshly ground black pepper

1 tablespoon balsamic vinegar

2 bell peppers of different colors, sliced into strips

2 tablespoons torn fresh basil or flat-leaf (Italian) parsley

1. Set one oven rack about 4 inches below the broiler element. Preheat the oven broiler to high. 2. Cover a large, rimmed baking sheet with aluminum foil. Place a wire cooling rack on top of the foil and coat the rack with nonstick cooking spray. Set aside. 3. Add half the mushrooms to a food processor and pulse about 15 times, until finely chopped but not puréed, similar to the texture of ground meat. Repeat with the remaining mushrooms. 4. Heat 1 tablespoon of oil in a large skillet over medium-high heat. Add the chopped mushrooms and cook for 2 to 3 minutes, stirring occasionally, until they have cooked down and some of their liquid has evaporated. Remove from the heat. 5. In a large bowl, combine the ground beef with the cooked mushrooms, garlic, ¼ teaspoon of salt, and pepper. Mix gently using your hands. Form the meat into 8 small (½-inch-thick) patties, and place on the prepared rack, making two lines of 4 patties down the center of the pan. 6. Put the pan in the oven so the broiler heating element is directly over as many burgers as possible. Broil for 4 minutes. Flip the burgers and rearrange them so any burgers not getting brown are nearer to the heat source. Broil for 3 to 4 more minutes, or until the internal temperature of the meat is 160°F on a meat thermometer. Watch carefully to prevent burning. 7. While the burgers are cooking, in a large bowl, whisk together the remaining 1 tablespoon of oil, vinegar, and remaining ¼ teaspoon of salt. Add the peppers and basil, and stir gently to coat with the dressing. Serve the sliders with the pepper slaw as a topping or on the side.

Per Serving: Calories 237; Fat 12.74g; Sodium 372mg; Carbs 5.39g; Fiber 1g; Sugar 2.9g; Protein 26.67g

Lemon Rosemary Lamb Chops

Prep Time: 1 hour 35 minutes | Cook Time: 10 minutes | Serves: 6

4 large cloves garlic

1 cup lemon juice

⅓ cup fresh rosemary

1 cup extra-virgin olive oil

1½ teaspoons salt

1 teaspoon freshly ground black pepper

6 1-inch-thick lamb chops

1. In a blender or food processor, blend the garlic, rosemary, olive oil, salt, lemon juice, and black pepper for 15 seconds. Set aside. 2. Put the lamb chops in a large plastic zip-top bag or container. Cover the lamb with two-thirds of the rosemary dressing, making sure that all of the lamb chops are coated with the dressing. Let the lamb marinate in the fridge for 1 hour. 3. When you are almost ready to eat, take the lamb chops out of the fridge and let them sit on the counter-top for 20 minutes. Preheat a grill, grill pan, or lightly oiled skillet to high heat. 4. Cook the lamb chops for 3 minutes on each side. To serve, drizzle the lamb with the remaining dressing.

Per Serving: Calories 500; Fat 43.73g; Sodium 900mg; Carbs 4.02g; Fiber 0.5g; Sugar 1.05g; Protein 23.56g

Tarragon Lamb Shanks with Beans and Carrots

Prep Time: 20 minutes | Cook Time: 10 hours | Serves: 6

4 (1½-pound) lamb shanks

One 19-ounce can cannellini or other white beans, rinsed and drained

2 medium-sized carrots, diced

1 large yellow onion, chopped

1 large stalk celery, chopped

2 cloves garlic, thinly sliced

2 teaspoons tarragon

½ teaspoon sea salt

¼ teaspoon black pepper

One 28-ounce can diced tomatoes, with the juice

1. Trim the fat from the lamb shanks. 2. Put the beans, onion, celery, carrots, and garlic in the slow cooker and stir to combine. 3. Place lamb shanks on the bean mixture, and sprinkle with the tarragon, salt, and pepper. 4. Pour the tomatoes over the lamb. Cover and cook on high for 1 hour. 5. Reduce heat to low, and cook 9 hours or until the lamb is very tender. Remove the lamb shanks from slow cooker and place on a plate. 6. Pour the bean mixture through a colander or sieve over a bowl, reserving the liquid. Let the liquid stand for 5 minutes. Skim the fat from the surface of the liquid. Return the bean mixture to the liquid. Return to the slow cooker. 7. Remove the lamb from the bones. Discard the bones. Return the lamb to the slow cooker. Cover and cook to reheat, about 15 minutes. 8. Serve the lamb hot with the bean mixture.

Per Serving: Calories 295; Fat 7.12g; Sodium 648mg; Carbs 26.92g; Fiber 3.4g; Sugar 5.02g; Protein 32.84g

Spanish Pepper Steak with Onions

Prep Time: 10 minutes | Cook Time: 20 minutes | Serves: 4

1 pound beef fillet

1 tablespoon smoked paprika

¼ cup extra-virgin olive oil

3 tablespoons garlic, minced

1½ teaspoons salt

1 large onion, sliced

2 large bell peppers, any color, sliced

1. Cut the beef into thin strips. Season with the paprika. 2. In a large skillet over medium heat, cook the olive oil, beef, garlic, and salt for 7 minutes, using tongs to toss. 3. Turn the heat to low and add in the onion. Cook for 7 minutes. 4. Add the bell peppers and cook for 6 minutes. 5. Serve.

Per Serving: Calories 197; Fat 7.66g; Sodium 975mg; Carbs 8.66g; Fiber 1.7g; Sugar 2.98g; Protein 24.78g

Lebanese Stuffed Cabbage Rolls

Prep Time: 15 minutes | Cook Time: 33 minutes | Serves: 4

1 head green cabbage

1 pound lean ground beef

½ cup long-grain brown rice

4 garlic cloves, minced

1 teaspoon salt

½ teaspoon black pepper

1 teaspoon ground cinnamon

2 tablespoons chopped fresh mint

Juice of 1 lemon

Olive oil cooking spray

½ cup beef broth

1 tablespoon olive oil

1. Cut the cabbage in half and remove the core. Remove 12 of the larger leaves to use for the cabbage rolls. 2. Bring a large pot of salted water to a boil, then drop the cabbage leaves into the water, boiling them for 3 minutes. Remove from the water and set aside. 3. In a large bowl, combine the ground beef, rice, pepper, cinnamon, garlic, salt, mint, and lemon juice, and mix together until combined. Divide this mixture into 12 equal portions. 4. Preheat the air fryer to 360°F. Lightly coat a small casserole dish with olive oil cooking spray. 5. Arrange a cabbage leaf on a clean work surface. Place a spoonful of the beef mixture on one side of the leaf, leaving space on all other sides. Fold the two perpendicular sides inward and then roll forward, tucking tightly as rolled (similar to a burrito roll). Place the finished rolls into the baking dish, stacking them on top of each other if needed. 6. Pour the beef broth over the top of the cabbage rolls so that it soaks down between them, and then brush the tops with the olive oil. 7. Place the casserole dish into the air fryer basket and bake for 30 minutes.

Per Serving: Calories 330; Fat 10.11g; Sodium 737mg; Carbs 33.62g; Fiber 4.4g; Sugar 5.97g; Protein 28.65g

Baked Lamb Kofta Meatballs

Prep Time: 15 minutes | Cook Time: 30 minutes | Serves: 2

¼ cup walnuts

½ small onion

1 garlic clove

1 roasted piquillo pepper

2 tablespoons fresh parsley

2 tablespoons fresh mint

¼ teaspoon salt

¼ teaspoon cumin

¼ teaspoon allspice

Pinch cayenne pepper

8 ounces lean ground lamb

1. Preheat the oven to 350°F and set the rack to the middle position. Line a baking sheet with foil. 2. In a food processor, combine the walnuts, roasted pepper, parsley, onion, garlic, mint, salt, allspice, cumin, and cayenne pepper. Pulse about 10 times to combine everything. 3. Transfer the spice mixture to the bowl and add the lamb. With your hands or a spatula, mix the spices into the lamb. 4. Roll into 1½-inch balls (about the size of golf balls). 5. Place the meatballs on the foil-lined baking sheet and bake for 30 minutes, or until cooked to an internal temperature of 160°F.

Per Serving: Calories 308; Fat 20.86g; Sodium 361mg; Carbs 6.65g; Fiber 1.8g; Sugar 2.25g; Protein 25.6g

Tender Beef Kebabs

Prep Time: 15 minutes | Cook Time: 10 minutes | Serves: 6

2 pounds beef fillet

1½ teaspoons salt

1 teaspoon freshly ground black pepper

½ teaspoon ground allspice

½ teaspoon ground nutmeg

⅓ cup extra-virgin olive oil

1 large onion, cut into 8 quarters

1 large red bell pepper, cut into 1-inch cubes

1. Preheat a grill, grill pan, or lightly oiled skillet to high heat. 2. Cut the beef into 1-inch cubes and put them in a large bowl. 3. In a small bowl, mix together the salt, allspice, black pepper, and nutmeg. 4. Pour the olive oil over the beef and toss to coat the beef. Then evenly sprinkle the seasoning over the beef and toss to coat all pieces. 5. Skewer the beef, alternating every 1 or 2 pieces with a piece of onion or bell pepper. 6. To cook, place the skewers on the grill or skillet, and turn every 2 to 3 minutes until all sides have cooked to desired doneness, 6 minutes for medium-rare, 8 minutes for well done. Serve warm.

Per Serving: Calories 397; Fat 25.69g; Sodium 854mg; Carbs 4.2g; Fiber 0.9g; Sugar 1.74g; Protein 38.09g

Air Fryer Lamb Kofta with Mint-Yogurt Sauce

Prep Time: 40 minutes | Cook Time: 10 minutes | Serves: 6

For the Kofta:

1 pound ground lamb

¼ cup fresh parsley, roughly chopped

2 garlic cloves, minced

¼ white onion, diced

1 teaspoon salt

1 teaspoon ground cumin

½ teaspoon black pepper

¼ teaspoon ground cinnamon

¼ teaspoon ground allspice

¼ teaspoon cayenne pepper

¼ teaspoon ground ginger

3 tablespoons olive oil, divided

For the Mint-Yogurt Sauce:

1 cup nonfat plain Greek yogurt

½ cup fresh mint, chopped

1 garlic clove, minced

2 tablespoons lemon juice

½ teaspoon ground cumin

¼ teaspoon cayenne pepper

¼ teaspoon salt

¼ teaspoon black pepper

To make the kofta: 1. Preheat the air fryer to 360°F. 2. In a large bowl, combine the ground lamb with the parsley, onion, garlic, and all the spices and 2 tablespoons olive oil, then mix until well combined and the spices are distributed evenly. 3. Divide the mixture into 4 equal quantities, and roll each into a long oval (or any shape you prefer) by hand. 4. Brush the remaining 1 tablespoon of olive oil over the lamb ovals, place them in an even layer in the air fryer basket, and roast for 10 minutes, or until the internal temperature reaches 145°F.

To make the mint-yogurt sauce: 1. While the kofta is cooking, mix together the ingredients for the yogurt sauce and set aside. 2. Serve each kofta with a generous serving of mint sauce for dipping.

Per Serving: Calories 229; Fat 16.45g; Sodium 539mg; Carbs 3.25g; Fiber 0.7g; Sugar 1.04g; Protein 17.9g

Chapter 7 Fish and Seafood Recipes

Baked Grouper with Tomatoes and Olives

Prep Time: 5 minutes | Cook Time: 12 minutes | Serves: 4

4 grouper fillets

½ teaspoon salt

3 garlic cloves, minced

1 tomato, sliced

¼ cup sliced Kalamata olives

¼ cup fresh dill, roughly chopped

Juice of 1 lemon

¼ cup olive oil

1. Preheat the air fryer to 380°F. 2. Season the grouper fillets on all sides with the salt, then place into the air fryer basket and top with the minced garlic, olives, tomato slices, and fresh dill. 3. Drizzle the lemon juice and olive oil over the top of the grouper, then bake for 10 to 12 minutes, or until the internal temperature reaches 145°F.

Per Serving: Calories 379; Fat 17.15g; Sodium 492mg; Carbs 3.33g; Fiber 0.7g; Sugar 1.13g; Protein 50.74g

Baked Lemon Swordfish with Herbs

Prep Time: 10 minutes | Cook Time: 20 minutes | Serves: 4

Olive oil spray

1 cup fresh Italian parsley

¼ cup fresh thyme

¼ cup lemon juice

2 cloves garlic

¼ cup extra-virgin olive oil

½ teaspoon salt

4 swordfish steaks (each 5 to 7 ounces)

1. Preheat the oven to 450°F. Grease a large baking dish with olive oil spray. 2. In a food processor, pulse the parsley, thyme, garlic, olive oil, lemon juice, and salt 10 times. 3. Place the swordfish in the prepared baking dish. Spoon the parsley mixture over the steaks. 4. Put the fish in the oven to bake for 17 to 20 minutes.

Per Serving: Calories 380; Fat 25.26g; Sodium 438mg; Carbs 3.08g; Fiber 0.9g; Sugar 0.53g; Protein 34.17g

Cilantro-Lemon Shrimp

Prep Time: 20 minutes | Cook Time: 10 minutes | Serves: 4

⅓ cup lemon juice

4 garlic cloves

1 cup fresh cilantro leaves

½ teaspoon ground coriander

3 tablespoons extra-virgin olive oil

1 teaspoon salt

1½ pounds large shrimp (21-25), deveined and shells removed

1. In a food processor, pulse the lemon juice, cilantro, coriander, garlic, olive oil, and salt 10 times. 2. Put the shrimp in a bowl or plastic zip-top bag, pour in the cilantro marinade, and let sit for 15 minutes. 3. Preheat a skillet on high heat. 4. Put the shrimp and marinade in the skillet. Cook the shrimp for 3 minutes on each side. Serve warm.

Per Serving: Calories 220; Fat 11.93g; Sodium 1547mg; Carbs 4.11g; Fiber 0.2g; Sugar 0.58g; Protein 23.51g

Seared Scallops with Vegetables

Prep Time: 5 minutes | Cook Time: 12 minutes | Serves: 4

2 tablespoons extra-virgin olive oil, divided
12 large sea scallops (about 1 pound), side muscles removed, patted dry
⅛ teaspoon freshly ground black pepper
8 ounces asparagus, ends trimmed
1 cup snap peas

1 cup baby carrots, halved lengthwise
1 medium shallot, finely chopped
2 garlic cloves, minced
¼ cup reduced-sodium vegetable stock
6 ounces baby spinach

1. In a large skillet, heat 1 tablespoon of olive oil over medium-high heat. Sprinkle the scallops with the black pepper and add them to the skillet. Cook for about 2 minutes per side, or until just golden. Transfer them to a plate and cover loosely with aluminum foil to keep them warm. 2. Add the remaining 1 tablespoon of olive oil to the skillet, along with the asparagus, snap peas, shallot, carrots, and garlic. Cook for about 4 minutes, stirring often, or until the vegetables are tender-crisp. Add the vegetable stock and spinach and cook for 1 to 2 minutes, or until the spinach is slightly wilted. 3. Serve the vegetables alongside the scallops. 4. Refrigerate the leftovers in an airtight container for up to 5 days.
Per Serving: Calories 172; Fat 7.67g; Sodium 446mg; Carbs 12.74g; Fiber 3.7g; Sugar 3.82g; Protein 14.49g

Sardine Stuffed Peppers

Prep Time: 10 minutes | Cook Time: 20-25 minutes | Serves: 2

2 red peppers
2 cans of sardines or salmon or tuna, weighing about 175g (6oz)
8 cherry tomatoes, halved
10 black olives, stoned (optional)
8 anchovy fillets in oil (optional)

4 teaspoons baby capers, drained and rinsed (optional)
1 heaped teaspoon dried oregano (optional)
A pinch of chilli flakes (optional)
2 tablespoons extra virgin olive oil
Salt and freshly ground black pepper

1. Preheat the oven to 220°C/200°C fan/425°F/gas mark 7. 2. Halve the pepper lengthways through the stalk. Pick out the white membrane and seeds. Drain the sardines in a sieve. 3. Put the peppers in an ovenproof dish or roasting tray. Layer up the sardines, tomatoes and olives, capers, oregano, anchovies, and chilli flakes, if using, into each pepper cavity with a little seasoning (as the anchovies are salty) and oil as you go. Finish with a drizzle of oil and cook for 20–25 minutes or until the peppers are tender and the filling is piping hot. 4. Serve alone or with the green salad.
Per Serving: Calories 343; Fat 23.92g; Sodium 2169mg; Carbs 8.7g; Fiber 2.9g; Sugar 4.34g; Protein 24.77g

Thyme Salmon with Orange and Fennel

Prep Time: 15 minutes | Cook Time: 12-15 minutes | Serves: 4

Approx. 700g (1lb 9oz) fennel bulbs (untrimmed weight)

4 tablespoons extra virgin olive oil

1 medium orange

4 x 120g (4½oz) salmon steaks

1 medium brown onion, sliced into half-moons

4 tablespoons white wine or water (optional)

A few sprigs of thyme or 1 teaspoon dried thyme or rosemary

Salt and freshly ground black pepper

1. Trim the tough stalks and base away from the fennel, reserving a few feathery green fronds to serve. Cut the bulbs into 1cm (½in) slices from top to base. Cook in boiling water for 5 minutes, then drain in a sieve and set aside. 2. Preheat the oven to 200°C/180°C fan/400°F/gas mark 6 and brush a roasting tray with a little of the oil. 3. Use a sharp knife to cut away the peel from the orange, trying to waste as little flesh as possible. Then cut the orange in half and rest each half on a board flat-side down. Cut each half into 6–7 segments. 4. Season the salmon all over and lay on the prepared tray. Put the drained fennel, onion, and orange around the fish and season with the salt and pepper. Pour the wine over the vegetables, if using. Drizzle the remaining oil over the fish and scatter the thyme over everything. Bake for 12–15 minutes or until the fish is cooked through. 5. Serve straight away scattered with the reserved fennel fronds.

Per Serving: Calories 241; Fat 15.15g; Sodium 400mg; Carbs 19.97g; Fiber 6.8g; Sugar 11.02g; Protein 9.26g

Fried Fishcakes with Zucchini Salad

Prep Time: 10 minutes | Cook Time: 4 minutes | Serves: 4

Approx. 520g (1lb 3oz) white fish fillets, such as haddock, cod or coley

1 medium onion, roughly chopped

10g (¼oz) mint leaves

For the Zucchini Salad:

2 medium zucchinis, weighing about 275g (9¾oz)

2 tablespoons extra virgin olive oil

Juice of ½ lemon

10g (¼oz) coriander or flat-leaf parsley, stalks and leaves roughly chopped

2 tablespoons extra virgin olive oil, ghee or coconut oil

1 mild red chilli, finely sliced, or a pinch of chilli flakes

1 garlic clove, grated

Salt and freshly ground black pepper

1. Cut the fish fillets into 3 pieces and pop them into a food processor, squeezing out any juices if the fish was frozen. Add the onion, herbs and 1 teaspoon of salt and whizz to form a rough paste. Divide the mixture into 8 and use your hands to form even-sized fishcakes. 2. Fry the fishcakes in the oil over a medium-high heat for about 4 minutes on each side or until lightly browned and cooked through. 3. Meanwhile, make the salad. Slice the zucchini with a vegetable peeler. Add the remaining ingredients and stir through. Taste and adjust the seasoning and serve with the fishcakes.

Per Serving: Calories 244; Fat 14.61g; Sodium 539mg; Carbs 7.38g; Fiber 2g; Sugar 1.37g; Protein 22.3g

Swordfish in Citrusy Tarragon Butter

Prep Time: 5 minutes | Cook Time: 20 minutes | Serves: 4

1 pound swordfish steaks, cut into 2-inch pieces

1 teaspoon salt

¼ teaspoon freshly ground black pepper

¼ cup extra-virgin olive oil, plus 2 tablespoons, divided

2 tablespoons unsalted butter

Zest and juice of 2 clementines

Zest and juice of 1 lemon

2 tablespoons chopped fresh tarragon

Sautéed greens, riced cauliflower, or zucchini noodles, for serving

1. In a bowl, toss the swordfish with salt and pepper. 2. In a large skillet, heat ¼ cup olive oil over medium-high heat. Add the swordfish chunks to the hot oil and sear on all sides, 2 to 3 minutes per side, until they are lightly golden brown. Using a slotted spoon, remove the fish from the pan and keep warm. 3. Add the remaining 2 tablespoons olive oil and butter to the oil already in the pan and return the heat to medium-low. Once the butter has melted, whisk in the clementine and lemon zests and juices, along with the tarragon. Season with the salt. Return the fish pieces to the pan and toss to coat in the butter sauce. 4. Serve the fish drizzled with the sauce over sautéed greens, riced cauliflower, or zucchini noodles.

Per Serving: Calories 341; Fat 25.05g; Sodium 677mg; Carbs 5.82g; Fiber 0.8g; Sugar 3.7g; Protein 23.1g

Classic Escabeche

Prep Time: 10 minutes | Cook Time: 20 minutes | Serves: 4

1 pound wild-caught Spanish mackerel fillets, cut into four pieces

1 teaspoon salt

½ teaspoon freshly ground black pepper

8 tablespoons extra-virgin olive oil, divided

1 bunch asparagus, trimmed and cut into 2-inch pieces

1 (13.75-ounce) can artichoke hearts, drained and quartered

4 large garlic cloves, peeled and crushed

2 bay leaves

¼ cup red wine vinegar

½ teaspoon smoked paprika

1. Sprinkle the fillets with salt and pepper and let sit at room temperature for 5 minutes. 2. In a large skillet, heat 2 tablespoons olive oil over medium-high heat. Add the fish, skin-side up, and cook 5 minutes. Flip and continuing cooking for 5 minutes on the other side, until browned and cooked through. Transfer to a serving dish, pour the cooking oil over the fish, and cover to keep warm. 3. Heat the remaining 6 tablespoons olive oil in the same skillet over medium heat. Add the asparagus, garlic, artichokes, and bay leaves and sauté until the vegetables are tender, 6 to 8 minutes. 4. Using a slotted spoon, top the fish with the cooked vegetables, reserving the oil in the skillet. Add the vinegar and paprika to the oil and whisk to combine well. Pour the vinaigrette over the fish and vegetables and let sit at room temperature for at least 15 minutes, or marinate in the refrigerator up to 24 hours for a deeper flavor. Remove the bay leaf before serving.

Per Serving: Calories 406; Fat 29.59g; Sodium 783mg; Carbs 9.6g; Fiber 5.3g; Sugar 2.49g; Protein 26.65g

Garlicky Shrimp Stir-Fry with Mushrooms

Prep Time: 10 minutes | Cook Time: 15 minutes | Serves: 4

1 pound peeled and deveined fresh shrimp

1 teaspoon salt

1 cup extra-virgin olive oil

8 large garlic cloves, thinly sliced

4 ounces sliced mushrooms (shiitake, baby bella, or button)

½ teaspoon red pepper flakes

¼ cup chopped fresh flat-leaf Italian parsley

Zucchini noodles or riced cauliflower, for serving

1. Rinse the shrimp and pat dry. Place in a small bowl and sprinkle with the salt. 2. In a large rimmed, thick skillet, heat the olive oil over medium-low heat. Add the garlic and heat until very fragrant, 3 to 4 minutes, reducing the heat if the garlic starts to burn. 3. Add the mushrooms and sauté for 5 minutes, until softened. Add the shrimp and red pepper flakes and sauté until the shrimp begins to turn pink, another 3 to 4 minutes. 4. Remove from the heat and stir in the parsley. Serve over the zucchini noodles or riced cauliflower.

Per Serving: Calories 594; Fat 54.82g; Sodium 723mg; Carbs 4.27g; Fiber 1g; Sugar 0.79g; Protein 23.95g

Herbed Tuna Steak in Olive Oil

Prep Time: 5 minutes | Cook Time: 45 minutes | Serves: 4

1 cup extra-virgin olive oil, plus more if needed

4 (3- to 4-inch) sprigs fresh rosemary

8 (3- to 4-inch) sprigs fresh thyme

2 large garlic cloves, thinly sliced

2 (2-inch) strips lemon zest

1 teaspoon salt

½ teaspoon freshly ground black pepper

1 pound fresh tuna steaks (about 1 inch thick)

1. Select a thick pot just large enough to fit the tuna in a single layer on the bottom. The larger the pot, the more olive oil you will need to use. Combine the olive oil, rosemary, lemon zest, salt, thyme, garlic, and pepper over medium-low heat and cook until warm and fragrant, 20 to 25 minutes, lowering the heat if it begins to smoke. 2. Remove from the heat and allow to cool for 25 to 30 minutes, until warm but not hot. 3. Add the tuna to the bottom of the pan, adding additional oil if needed so that tuna is fully submerged, and return to medium-low heat. Cook for 5 to 10 minutes, or until the oil heats back up and is warm and fragrant but not smoking. Lower the heat if it gets too hot. 4. Remove the pot from the heat and let the tuna cook in warm oil 4 to 5 minutes, to your desired level of doneness. For a tuna that is rare in the center, cook for 2 to 3 minutes. 5. Remove from the oil and serve warm, drizzling 2 to 3 tablespoons seasoned oil over the tuna. 6. To store for later use, remove the tuna from the oil and place in a container with a lid. Allow tuna and oil to cool separately. When both have cooled, remove the herb stems with a slotted spoon and pour the cooking oil over the tuna. Cover and store in the refrigerator for up to 1 week. Bring to room temperature to allow the oil to liquify before serving.

Per Serving: Calories 653; Fat 59.76g; Sodium 628mg; Carbs 3.09g; Fiber 0.6g; Sugar 0.62g; Protein 26.81g

Lemon Snapper Baked in Parchment

Prep Time: 15 minutes | Cook Time: 15 minutes | Serves: 4

1¼ pounds fresh red snapper fillet, cut into two equal pieces

2 lemons, thinly sliced

6 to 8 sprigs fresh rosemary, stems removed or 1 to 2 tablespoons dried rosemary

½ cup extra-virgin olive oil

6 garlic cloves, thinly sliced

1 teaspoon salt

½ teaspoon freshly ground black pepper

1. Preheat the oven to 425°F. 2. Place two large sheets of parchment (about twice the size of each piece of fish) on the counter. Place 1 piece of fish in the center of each sheet. 3. Top the fish pieces with lemon slices and rosemary leaves. 4. In a small bowl, combine the olive oil, salt, garlic, and pepper. Drizzle the oil over each piece of fish. 5. Top each piece of fish with a second large sheet of parchment and starting on a long side, fold the paper up to about 1 inch from the fish. Repeat on the remaining sides, going in a clockwise direction. Fold in each corner once to secure. 6. Place both parchment pouches on a baking sheet and bake until the fish is cooked through, 10 to 12 minutes.

Per Serving: Calories 397; Fat 29.14g; Sodium 674mg; Carbs 3.86g; Fiber 0.6g; Sugar 0.65g; Protein 29.56g

Garlic Shrimp with Tomatoes and Olives

Prep Time: 15 minutes | Cook Time: 20 minutes | Serves: 4

1 pound large shrimp (26 to 30 per pound), peeled and deveined

2 tablespoons extra-virgin olive oil, divided, plus extra for drizzling

5 garlic cloves, minced, divided

1 teaspoon grated lemon zest

½ teaspoon table salt, divided

⅛ teaspoon pepper

1 red or green bell pepper, stemmed, seeded, and chopped

1 small onion, chopped

1 tablespoon ras el hanout

½ teaspoon ground ginger

1 (28-ounce) can whole peeled tomatoes, drained with juice reserved, chopped coarse

¼ cup pitted brine-cured green or black olives, chopped coarse

2 tablespoons coarsely chopped fresh parsley

2 scallions, sliced thin on bias

1. Toss the shrimp with 1 tablespoon oil, 1 teaspoon garlic, lemon zest, ¼ teaspoon salt, and pepper; refrigerate until ready to use. 2. Using the highest sauté function, heat the remaining 1 tablespoon oil in the instant pot until shimmering. Add the bell pepper, onion, and remaining ¼ teaspoon salt and cook until the vegetables are softened, about 5 minutes. Stir in the remaining garlic, ras el hanout, and ginger and cook until fragrant, about 30 seconds. Stir in the tomatoes and reserved juice. 3. Lock the lid in place and close the pressure release valve. Set to the high pressure cook function and cook for 15 minutes. Turn off the instant pot and quickly release pressure. Carefully remove the lid, ensuring the steam escapes away from you. 4. Stir the shrimp into the tomato mixture, cover, and allow to sit until opaque throughout, 5 to 7 minutes. Stir in the olives and parsley and season with the salt and pepper to taste. Sprinkle individual portions with the scallions and drizzle with extra oil before serving.

Per Serving: Calories 217; Fat 8.04g; Sodium 662mg; Carbs 12.99g; Fiber 5.3g; Sugar 7.63g; Protein 25.39g

Easy Cod with Parsley Pistou

Prep Time: 15 minutes | Cook Time: 10 minutes | Serves: 4

1 cup packed roughly chopped fresh flat-leaf Italian parsley

1 to 2 small garlic cloves, minced

Zest and juice of 1 lemon

1 teaspoon salt

½ teaspoon freshly ground black pepper

1 cup extra-virgin olive oil, divided

1 pound cod fillets, cut into 4 equal-sized pieces

1. In a food processer, combine the parsley, lemon zest and juice, salt, garlic, and pepper. Pulse to chop well. 2. While the food processor is running, slowly stream in ¾ cup olive oil until well combined. Set aside. 3. In a large skillet, heat the remaining ¼ cup olive oil over medium-high heat. Add the cod fillets, cover, and cook 4 to 5 minutes on each side, or until cooked through. Thicker fillets may require a bit more cooking time. Remove from the heat and keep warm. 4. Add the pistou to the skillet and heat over medium-low heat. Return the cooked fish to the skillet, flipping to coat in the sauce. Serve warm, covered with pistou.

Per Serving: Calories 566; Fat 54.63g; Sodium 935mg; Carbs 2.22g; Fiber 0.6g; Sugar 0.4g; Protein 17.88g

Braised Striped Bass with Zucchini and Tomatoes

Prep Time: 20 minutes | Cook Time: 30 minutes | Serves: 4

2 tablespoons extra-virgin olive oil, divided, plus extra for drizzling

3 zucchinis (8 ounces each), halved lengthwise and sliced ¼ inch thick

1 onion, chopped

¾ teaspoon table salt, divided

3 garlic cloves, minced

1 teaspoon minced fresh oregano or ¼ teaspoon dried

¼ teaspoon red pepper flakes

1 (28-ounce) can whole peeled tomatoes, drained with juice reserved, halved

1½ pounds skinless striped bass, 1½ inches thick, cut into 2-inch pieces

¼ teaspoon pepper

2 tablespoons chopped pitted Kalamata olives

2 tablespoons shredded fresh mint

1. Using the highest sauté function, heat 1 tablespoon oil in the instant pot for 5 minutes (or until just smoking). Add the zucchini and cook until tender, about 5 minutes. Transfer to a bowl and set aside. 2. Add the remaining 1 tablespoon oil, onion, and ¼ teaspoon salt to a now-empty pot and cook, using the highest sauté function, until the onion is softened, about 5 minutes. Stir in the garlic, oregano, and pepper flakes and cook until fragrant, about 30 seconds. Stir in the tomatoes and reserved juice. 3. Sprinkle the bass with remaining ½ teaspoon salt and pepper. Nestle the bass into tomato mixture and spoon some of cooking liquid on top of pieces. Lock the lid in place and close the pressure release valve. Set to the high pressure cook function and set cook time for 10 minutes. Once the instant pot has reached pressure, immediately turn off the pot and quickly release pressure. Carefully remove the lid, ensuring the steam escapes away from you. 4. Transfer the bass to a plate, tent with aluminum foil, and let rest while finishing vegetables. Stir the zucchini into the pot and let sit until heated through, about 5 minutes. Stir in the olives and season with the salt and pepper to taste. Serve the bass with the vegetables, sprinkling individual portions with the mint and drizzling with extra oil.

Per Serving: Calories 313; Fat 12.42g; Sodium 819mg; Carbs 16.11g; Fiber 6.5g; Sugar 6.27g; Protein 36.87g

Balsamic Fish with Green Beans and Tomatoes

Prep Time: 10 minutes | Cook Time: 10 minutes | Serves: 4

Nonstick cooking spray

2 tablespoons extra-virgin olive oil

1 tablespoon balsamic vinegar

4 (4-ounce) fish fillets, such as cod or tilapia (½ inch thick)

2½ cups green beans (about 12 ounces)

1 pint cherry or grape tomatoes (about 2 cups)

1. Preheat the oven to 400°F. Coat two large, rimmed baking sheets with nonstick cooking spray. 2. In a small bowl, whisk together the oil and vinegar. Set aside. 3. Place two pieces of fish on each baking sheet. 4. In a large bowl, combine the beans and tomatoes. Pour in the oil and vinegar, and toss gently to coat. Pour half of the green bean mixture over the fish on one baking sheet, and the remaining half over the fish on the other. Turn the fish over, and rub it in the oil mixture to coat. Spread the vegetables evenly on the baking sheets so hot air can circulate around them. 5. Bake for 5 to 8 minutes, until the fish is just opaque and not translucent. The fish is done and ready to serve when it just starts to separate into flakes (chunks) when pressed gently with a fork.

Per Serving: Calories 176; Fat 7.86g; Sodium 350mg; Carbs 7.73g; Fiber 2.7g; Sugar 3.3g; Protein 19.06g

Garlic Salmon with Broccoli Rabe and White Beans

Prep Time: 20 minutes | Cook Time: 10 minutes | Serves: 4

2 tablespoons extra-virgin olive oil, plus extra for drizzling

4 garlic cloves, sliced thin

½ cup chicken or vegetable broth

¼ teaspoon red pepper flakes

1 lemon, sliced ¼ inch thick, plus lemon wedges for serving

4 (6-ounce) skinless salmon fillets, 1½ inches thick

½ teaspoon table salt

¼ teaspoon pepper

1 pound broccoli rabe, trimmed and cut into 1-inch pieces

1 (15-ounce) can cannellini beans, rinsed

1. Using the highest sauté function, cook the oil and garlic in the instant pot until garlic is fragrant and light golden brown, about 3 minutes. Using slotted spoon, transfer the garlic to paper towel–lined plate and season with the salt to taste; set aside for serving. Turn off the instant pot, then stir in the broth and pepper flakes. 2. Fold sheet of aluminum foil into 16 by 6-inch sling. Arrange the lemon slices widthwise in 2 rows across center of sling. Sprinkle the flesh side of salmon with the salt and pepper, then arrange the skinned side down on top of lemon slices. Using sling, lower salmon into the instant pot; allow narrow edges of sling to rest along sides of insert. Lock the lid in place and close the pressure release valve. Set to the high pressure cook function and cook for 3 minutes. 3. Turn off the instant pot and quickly release pressure. Carefully remove the lid, ensuring the steam escapes away from you. Using sling, transfer the salmon to a large plate. Tent with foil and let rest while preparing the broccoli rabe mixture. 4. Stir the broccoli rabe and beans into cooking liquid, partially cover, and cook, using the highest sauté function, until the broccoli rabe is tender, about 5 minutes. Season with the salt and pepper to taste. Gently lift and tilt the salmon fillets with a spatula to remove lemon slices. Serve the salmon with broccoli rabe mixture and lemon wedges, sprinkling individual portions with the garlic chips and drizzling with the extra oil.

Per Serving: Calories 390; Fat 14.96g; Sodium 744mg; Carbs 21.28g; Fiber 7.3g; Sugar 1.48g; Protein 43.15g

Butter Scallops and Calamari

Prep Time: 5 minutes | Cook Time: 10 minutes | Serves: 4

8 ounces calamari steaks, cut into ½-inch-thick strips or rings

8 ounces sea scallops

1½ teaspoons salt, divided

1 teaspoon freshly ground black pepper

1 teaspoon garlic powder

⅓ cup extra-virgin olive oil

2 tablespoons butter

1. Place the calamari and scallops on several layers of paper towels and pat dry. Sprinkle with 1 teaspoon salt and allow to sit for 15 minutes at room temperature. Pat dry with additional paper towels. Sprinkle with pepper and garlic powder. 2. In a deep medium skillet, heat the olive oil and butter over medium-high heat. When the oil is hot but not smoking, add the scallops and calamari in a single layer to the skillet and sprinkle with the remaining ½ teaspoon salt. Cook 2 to 4 minutes on each side, depending on the size of the scallops, until just golden but still slightly opaque in center. 3. Using a slotted spoon, remove from the skillet and transfer to a serving platter. Allow the cooking oil to cool slightly and drizzle over the seafood before serving.

Per Serving: Calories 280; Fat 18g; Sodium 880mg; Carbs 3g; Fiber 0g; Sugar 0g; Protein 24g

Salmon with Garlic Mashed Cauliflower

Prep Time: 15 minutes | Cook Time: 10 minutes | Serves: 4

2 tablespoons extra-virgin olive oil

4 garlic cloves, peeled and smashed

½ cup chicken or vegetable broth

¾ teaspoon table salt, divided

1 large head cauliflower (3 pounds), cored and cut into 2-inch florets

4 (6-ounce) skinless salmon fillets, 1½ inches thick

½ teaspoon ras el hanout

½ teaspoon grated lemon zest

3 scallions, sliced thin

1 tablespoon sesame seeds, toasted

1. Using the highest sauté function, cook the oil and garlic in the instant pot until garlic is fragrant and light golden brown, about 3 minutes. Turn off the instant pot, then stir in the broth and ¼ teaspoon salt. Arrange the cauliflower in the pot in even layer. 2. Fold sheet of aluminum foil into 16 by 6-inch sling. Sprinkle flesh side of salmon with ras el hanout and remaining ½ teaspoon salt, then arrange skinned side down in center of sling. Using sling, lower salmon into the instant pot on top of cauliflower; allow narrow edges of sling to rest along sides of insert. Lock the lid in place and close the pressure release valve. Set to the high pressure cook function and cook for 2 minutes. 3. Turn off the instant pot and quickly release pressure. Carefully remove the lid, ensuring the steam escapes away from you. Using sling, transfer the salmon to a large plate. Tent with foil and let rest while finishing cauliflower. 4. Using a potato masher, mash the cauliflower mixture until no large chunks remain. Using the highest sauté function, cook the cauliflower, stirring often, until slightly thickened, about 3 minutes. Stir in the lemon zest and season with the salt and pepper to taste. Serve the salmon with the cauliflower, sprinkling individual portions with the scallions and sesame seeds.

Per Serving: Calories 355; Fat 15.88g; Sodium 649mg; Carbs 14.41g; Fiber 5g; Sugar 5.03g; Protein 39.81g

Mediterranean Grilled Shrimp Skewers

Prep Time: 20 minutes | Cook Time: 5 minutes | Serves: 4-6

2 tablespoons garlic, minced

½ cup lemon juice

3 tablespoons fresh Italian parsley, finely chopped

¼ cup extra-virgin olive oil

1 teaspoon salt

2 pounds jumbo shrimp (21-25), peeled and deveined

1. In a large bowl, mix the garlic, parsley, olive oil, lemon juice, and salt. 2. Add the shrimp to the bowl and toss to make sure all the pieces are coated with the marinade. Let the shrimp sit for 15 minutes. 3. Preheat a grill, grill pan, or lightly oiled skillet to high heat. While heating, thread about 5 to 6 pieces of shrimp onto each skewer. 4. Place the skewers on the grill, grill pan, or skillet and cook for 2 to 3 minutes on each side until cooked through. Serve warm.

Per Serving: Calories 261; Fat 11.82g; Sodium 683mg; Carbs 2.95g; Fiber 0.2g; Sugar 0.67g; Protein 36.84g

Lemon Cod with Tabbouleh Salad

Prep Time: 10 minutes | Cook Time: 6 minutes | Serves: 4

1 cup medium-grind bulgur, rinsed

1 teaspoon table salt, divided

1 lemon, sliced ¼ inch thick, plus 2 tablespoons juice

4 (6-ounce) skinless cod fillets, 1½ inches thick

3 tablespoons extra-virgin olive oil, divided, plus extra for drizzling

¼ teaspoon pepper

1 small shallot, minced

10 ounces cherry tomatoes, halved

1 cup chopped fresh parsley

½ cup chopped fresh mint

1. Arrange trivet included with the instant pot in base of insert and add ½ cup water. Fold sheet of aluminum foil into 16 by 6-inch sling, then rest 1½-quart round soufflé dish in center of sling. Combine 1 cup water, bulgur, and ½ teaspoon salt in the dish. Using sling, lower the soufflé dish into the pot and onto trivet; allow narrow edges of sling to rest along sides of insert. 2. Lock the lid in place and close the pressure release valve. Set to the high pressure cook function and cook for 3 minutes. Turn off the instant pot and quickly release pressure. Carefully remove the lid, ensuring the steam escapes away from you. Using sling, transfer the soufflé dish to wire rack; set aside to cool. Remove the trivet; do not discard sling or water in the pot. 3. Arrange the lemon slices widthwise in 2 rows across center of sling. Brush the cod with 1 tablespoon oil and sprinkle with the remaining ½ teaspoon salt and pepper. Arrange the cod skinned side down in even layer on top of lemon slices. Using sling, lower the cod into the instant pot; allow narrow edges of sling to rest along sides of insert. Lock the lid in place and close the pressure release valve. Set to the high pressure cook function and cook for 3 minutes. 4. Meanwhile, stir the remaining 2 tablespoons oil, lemon juice, and shallot together in a large bowl. Add the bulgur, tomatoes, parsley, and mint, and gently toss to combine. Season with the salt and pepper to taste. 5. Turn off the instant pot and quickly release pressure. Carefully remove the lid, ensuring the steam escapes away from you. Using sling, transfer the cod to a large plate. Gently lift and tilt the fillets with a spatula to remove the lemon slices. Serve the cod with the salad, drizzling individual portions with extra oil.

Per Serving: Calories 345; Fat 11.53g; Sodium 1114mg; Carbs 30.52g; Fiber 5.5g; Sugar 1.89g; Protein 31.22g

Roasted Branzino with Lemon and Herbs

Prep Time: 10 minutes | Cook Time: 20 minutes | Serves: 2

1 to 1½ pounds branzino, scaled and gutted
Salt
Freshly ground black pepper
1 tablespoon olive oil

1 lemon, sliced
3 garlic cloves, minced
¼ cup chopped fresh herbs (any mixture of oregano, thyme, parsley, and rosemary)

1. Preheat the oven to 425°F and set the rack to the middle position. 2. Lay the cleaned fish in a baking dish and make 4 to 5 slits in it, about 1½ inches apart. 3. Season the inside of the branzino with the salt and pepper and drizzle with the olive oil. 4. Fill the cavity of the fish with the lemon slices. Sprinkle the chopped garlic and herbs over the lemon and close the fish. 5. Roast the fish for 15 to 20 minutes, or until the flesh is opaque and it flakes apart easily. 6. Before eating, open the fish, remove the lemon slices, and carefully pull out the bone.
Per Serving: Calories 288; Fat 8.21g; Sodium 1187mg; Carbs 4.7g; Fiber 1g; Sugar 0.65g; Protein 46.97g

Moroccan Fish Tagine

Prep Time: 25 minutes | Cook Time: 22 minutes | Serves: 4

2 tablespoons extra-virgin olive oil, plus extra for drizzling
1 large onion, halved and sliced ¼ inch thick
1 pound carrots, peeled, halved lengthwise, and sliced ¼ inch thick
2 (2-inch) strips orange zest, plus 1 teaspoon grated zest
¾ teaspoon table salt, divided
2 tablespoons tomato paste
4 garlic cloves, minced, divided
1¼ teaspoons paprika

1 teaspoon ground cumin
¼ teaspoon red pepper flakes
¼ teaspoon saffron threads, crumbled
1 (8-ounce) bottle clam juice
1½ pounds skinless halibut fillets, 1½ inches thick, cut into 2-inch pieces
¼ cup pitted oil-cured black olives, quartered
2 tablespoons chopped fresh parsley
1 teaspoon sherry vinegar

1. Using the highest sauté function, heat the oil in the instant pot until shimmering. Add the onion, orange zest strips, carrots, and ¼ teaspoon salt, and cook until the vegetables are softened and lightly browned, 10 to 12 minutes. Stir in the tomato paste, three-quarters of garlic, pepper flakes, paprika, cumin, and saffron and cook until fragrant, about 30 seconds. Stir in the clam juice, scraping up any browned bits. 2. Sprinkle the halibut with remaining ½ teaspoon salt. Nestle the halibut into onion mixture and spoon some of cooking liquid on top of pieces. Lock the lid in place and close the pressure release valve. Set to the high pressure cook function and set cook time for 10 minutes. Once the instant pot has reached pressure, immediately turn off pot and quickly release pressure. 3. Discard the orange zest. Gently stir in the olives, parsley, vinegar, grated orange zest, and remaining garlic. Season with the salt and pepper to taste. Drizzle extra oil over individual portions before serving.
Per Serving: Calories 441; Fat 23.36g; Sodium 845mg; Carbs 24.19g; Fiber 4.9g; Sugar 9.97g; Protein 34.2g

Chapter 8 Soup and Stew Recipes

Lamb Chili Stew with Lentils

Prep Time: 10 minutes | Cook Time: 6 to 8 hours | Serves: 4

1 tablespoon extra-virgin olive oil

2 pounds raw ground lamb

1 (28-ounce) can no-salt-added crushed tomatoes

2½ cups water

1 onion, finely chopped

1 green bell pepper, seeded and diced

¾ cup dried lentils, any color

2 garlic cloves, minced

1 tablespoon chili powder

1 tablespoon ground cumin

1½ teaspoons sea salt

1 teaspoon dried oregano

½ teaspoon freshly ground black pepper

1. Heat the olive oil in a large skillet over medium-high heat. Add the ground lamb and cook for 3 to 5 minutes, breaking up the meat with a spoon, until it has browned and is no longer pink. Drain any grease and transfer the lamb to a slow cooker. 2. Add the tomatoes, water, onion, lentils, garlic, chili powder, bell pepper, cumin, salt, oregano, and black pepper to the lamb. Stir to mix well. 3. Cover the cooker and cook for 6 to 8 hours on Low heat, or until the lentils are tender. 4. Serve.

Per Serving: Calories 545; Fat 32.79g; Sodium 1088mg; Carbs 16.24g; Fiber 5.7g; Sugar 7g; Protein 50.18g

Hearty Slow Cooker Quinoa Beef Stew

Prep Time: 10 minutes | Cook Time: 4-8 hours | Serves: 6

1 tablespoon extra-virgin olive oil

1 pound lean stewing beef, cut into 1-inch cubes

1 medium yellow onion, diced

1 large carrot, diced

2 celery stalks, diced

3 garlic cloves, minced

4 cups reduced-sodium beef stock

1 (14½-ounce) can no-salt-added diced tomatoes

2 medium red potatoes, cut into ½-inch cubes

½ cup frozen peas

½ cup quinoa

3 bay leaves

½ teaspoon freshly ground black pepper

¼ teaspoon salt

1. In a large skillet, heat the olive oil over medium heat. Add the beef and cook until browned, 3 to 4 minutes. Add the onion, celery, carrot, and garlic and cook for 5 minutes, stirring occasionally. Transfer the ingredients to a slow cooker. 2. Stir in the beef stock, diced tomatoes with their juices, quinoa, bay leaves, potatoes, peas, pepper, and salt. Cover and cook on high for 3 to 4 hours or on low for 6 to 8 hours. Discard the bay leaves prior to serving. 3. Refrigerate any leftovers in an airtight container for up to 5 days.

Per Serving: Calories 290; Fat 9.45g; Sodium 510mg; Carbs 29.42g; Fiber 4.8g; Sugar 4.97g; Protein 23.64g

White Bean and Kale Soup

Prep Time: 10 minutes | Cook Time: 30 minutes | Serves: 6

1 tablespoon extra-virgin olive oil

1 medium yellow onion, diced

2 garlic cloves, minced

3 (15-ounce) cans reduced-sodium cannellini beans, drained and rinsed

4 cups reduced-sodium vegetable stock

2 cups water

4 cups stemmed and chopped kale

2 tablespoons freshly squeezed lemon juice

½ teaspoon paprika

½ teaspoon freshly ground black pepper

¼ teaspoon salt

1. In a large stockpot, heat the olive oil over medium-high heat. Add the onion and cook for 4 to 5 minutes, until it starts to turn translucent. Add the garlic and sauté for 30 to 60 seconds, or until fragrant. 2. Stir in the beans, kale, lemon juice, vegetable stock, water, paprika, pepper, and salt. Bring to a boil, reduce the heat to low, and simmer for 20 minutes, or until the kale is tender and slightly wilted. 3. Serve the soup hot.

Per Serving: Calories 270; Fat 4.96g; Sodium 792mg; Carbs 45.58g; Fiber 12.5g; Sugar 5.67g; Protein 13.41g

Red Lentil Soup

Prep Time: 5 minutes | Cook Time: 30 minutes | Serves: 6

2 tablespoons extra-virgin olive oil

1 medium yellow onion, diced

1 celery stalk, diced

3 garlic cloves, minced

1½ tablespoons tomato paste

5 cups reduced-sodium vegetable stock

2 cups water

1½ cups red lentils, rinsed

1 large carrot, diced

1 bay leaf

1 teaspoon ground cumin

1 teaspoon Italian seasoning

¼ teaspoon salt

¼ teaspoon freshly ground black pepper

3 tablespoons freshly squeezed lemon juice

2 teaspoons grated lemon zest

1. In a large stockpot, heat the olive oil over medium-high heat. Add the onion and celery and cook for about 5 minutes, or until just tender. Add the garlic and tomato paste and sauté for 1 minute. 2. Add the vegetable stock, water, bay leaf, cumin, lentils, carrot, Italian seasoning, salt, and black pepper. Bring to a boil, reduce the heat to low, and simmer for 20 minutes, or until the lentils are soft. 3. Remove from the heat, discard the bay leaf, and stir in the lemon juice and zest. Serve the soup hot. Refrigerate the leftovers in an airtight container for up to 5 days.

Per Serving: Calories 309; Fat 7.43g; Sodium 623mg; Carbs 47.86g; Fiber 8.7g; Sugar 5.07g; Protein 15.77g

Italian Beef Short Rib Stew

Prep Time: 15 minutes | Cook Time: 6 to 8 hours | Serves: 8

3 pounds boneless beef short ribs, cut into 1-inch pieces

1½ pounds red potatoes, quartered

4 carrots, cut into ½-inch cubes

4 ounces mushrooms, sliced

1 large onion, diced

1 (28-ounce) can no-salt-added diced tomatoes

1 cup low-sodium beef broth

2 garlic cloves, minced

1 tablespoon dried thyme

1½ teaspoons dried parsley

1½ teaspoons sea salt

½ teaspoon freshly ground black pepper

1. In a slow cooker, combine the short ribs, potatoes, onion, tomatoes, carrots, mushrooms, beef broth, garlic, thyme, parsley, salt, and pepper. Stir to mix well. 2. Cover the cooker and cook for 6 to 8 hours on Low heat.

Per Serving: Calories 385; Fat 16.15g; Sodium 736mg; Carbs 23.43g; Fiber 5g; Sugar 5.9g; Protein 38.55g

Spinach and Brown Rice Soup

Prep Time: 10 minutes | Cook Time: 55 minutes | Serves: 6

1 tablespoon olive oil

1 large onion, chopped

2 cloves garlic, minced

3 pounds spinach leaves, stems removed and leaves chopped

8 cups chicken broth

½ cup long-grain brown rice

Sea salt and freshly ground pepper, to taste

1. In a large Dutch oven over medium heat, heat the olive oil. 2. Add the onion and garlic and cook until the onions are soft and translucent, about 5 minutes. Add the spinach and stir. 3. Cover the pot and cook the spinach until wilted, about 3 more minutes. 4. Using a slotted spoon, remove the spinach and onions from the pot, leaving the liquid. 5. Put the spinach mixture in a blender or food processor, and process until smooth, then return to the pot. 6. Add the chicken broth and bring to a boil. 7. Add the rice, reduce the heat, and simmer until rice is cooked, about 45 minutes. 8. Season to taste. Serve hot.

Per Serving: Calories 160; Fat 4.28g; Sodium 1538mg; Carbs 24.31g; Fiber 6g; Sugar 3.5g; Protein 10.08g

Farro and White Bean Soup

Prep Time: 15 minutes | Cook Time: 2 hours | Serves: 8

2 tablespoons olive oil

1 medium onion, diced

1 celery stalk, diced

2 garlic cloves, minced

8 cups chicken broth or water

1 cup white beans, soaked overnight, rinsed, and drained

1 (14-ounce) can diced tomatoes, with juice

1 cup farro

½ teaspoon thyme

½ teaspoon freshly ground pepper

2 bay leaves

Sea salt and freshly ground pepper, to taste

1. Heat the olive oil in a large stockpot on medium-high heat. Sauté the onion, celery, and garlic cloves just until tender. 2. Add the broth or water, tomatoes, beans, farro, and seasonings, and bring to a simmer. 3. Cover and cook for 2 hours, or until the beans and farro are tender. Season with the sea salt and freshly ground pepper to taste.

Per Serving: Calories 233; Fat 4.58g; Sodium 1138mg; Carbs 39.48g; Fiber 9.1g; Sugar 3.76g; Protein 10.64g

Spiced Chicken Soup with Squash and Chickpeas

Prep Time: 15 minutes | Cook Time: 30 minutes | Serves: 6-8

2 tablespoons extra-virgin olive oil

1 onion, chopped

1¾ teaspoons table salt

2 tablespoons tomato paste

4 garlic cloves, minced

1 tablespoon ground coriander

1½ teaspoons ground cumin

1 teaspoon ground cardamom

½ teaspoon ground allspice

¼ teaspoon cayenne pepper

7 cups water, divided

2 (12-ounce) bone-in split chicken breasts, trimmed

4 (5- to 7-ounce) bone-in chicken thighs, trimmed

1½ pounds butternut squash, peeled, seeded, and cut into 1½-inch pieces (4 cups)

1 (15-ounce) can chickpeas, rinsed

½ cup chopped fresh cilantro

1. Using the highest sauté function, heat the oil in the instant pot until shimmering. Add the onion and salt and cook until the onion is softened, about 5 minutes. Stir in the tomato paste, garlic, coriander, cumin, cardamom, allspice, and cayenne and cook until fragrant, about 30 seconds. Stir in 5 cups water, scraping up any browned bits. Nestle the chicken breasts and thighs in the pot, then arrange the squash evenly around the chicken. 2. Lock the lid in place and close the pressure release valve. Set to the high pressure cook function and cook for 20 minutes. Turn off the instant pot and quickly release pressure. Carefully remove the lid, ensuring the steam escapes away from you. 3. Transfer the chicken to a cutting board, let cool slightly, then shred into bite-size pieces using 2 forks; discard skin and bones. 4. Using wide, shallow spoon, skim excess fat from surface of soup, then break the squash into bite-size pieces. Stir the chicken and any accumulated juices, chickpeas, and remaining 2 cups water into the soup and allow to sit until heated through, about 3 minutes. Stir in the cilantro and season with the salt and pepper to taste. Serve.

Per Serving: Calories 375; Fat 11.74g; Sodium 1130mg; Carbs 23.38g; Fiber 5.3g; Sugar 4.86g; Protein 46.98g

Simple Tomato Basil Soup

Prep Time: 10 minutes | Cook Time: 10 minutes | Serves: 2

¼ cup extra-virgin olive oil

2 garlic cloves, minced

1 (14.5-ounce) can plum tomatoes, whole or diced

1 cup vegetable broth

¼ cup chopped fresh basil

1. In a medium pot, heat the oil over medium heat, then add the garlic and cook for 2 minutes, until fragrant. 2. Meanwhile, in a bowl using an immersion blender or in a blender, puree the tomatoes and their juices. 3. Add the pureed tomatoes and broth to the pot and mix well. Simmer for 10 to 15 minutes. 4. Serve garnished with the basil.

Per Serving: Calories 325; Fat 28.46g; Sodium 295mg; Carbs 16.37g; Fiber 4g; Sugar 7.19g; Protein 4.22g

Beef Oxtail Soup with White Beans and Tomatoes

Prep Time: 20 minutes | Cook Time: 1 hour 10 minutes | Serves: 6-8

4 pounds oxtails, trimmed

1 teaspoon table salt

1 tablespoon extra-virgin olive oil

1 onion, chopped fine

2 carrots, peeled and chopped fine

¼ cup ground dried Aleppo pepper

6 garlic cloves, minced

2 tablespoons tomato paste

¾ teaspoon dried oregano

½ teaspoon ground cinnamon

½ teaspoon ground cumin

6 cups water

1 (28-ounce) can diced tomatoes, drained

1 (15-ounce) can navy beans, rinsed

1 tablespoon sherry vinegar

¼ cup chopped fresh parsley

½ preserved lemon, pulp and white pith removed, rind rinsed and minced (2 tablespoons)

1. Pat the oxtails dry with paper towels and sprinkle with the salt. Using the highest sauté function, heat the oil in the instant pot for 5 minutes (or until just smoking). Brown half of oxtails, 4 to 6 minutes per side; transfer to plate. Set aside the remaining uncooked oxtails. 2. Add the onion and carrots to fat left in the pot and cook, Using the highest sauté function, until softened, about 5 minutes. Stir in the Aleppo pepper, garlic, tomato paste, oregano, cinnamon, and cumin and cook until fragrant, about 30 seconds. Stir in water, scraping up any browned bits, then stir in the tomatoes. Nestle the remaining uncooked oxtails into the pot along with the browned oxtails and add any accumulated juices. 3. Lock the lid in place and close the pressure release valve. Set to the high pressure cook function and cook for 45 minutes. Turn off the instant pot and quickly release pressure. Carefully remove the lid, ensuring the steam escapes away from you. 4. Transfer the oxtails to a cutting board, let cool slightly, then shred into bite-size pieces using 2 forks; discard the bones and excess fat. Strain the broth through a fine-mesh strainer into a large container; return the solids to a now-empty pot. Using a wide, shallow spoon, skim excess fat from surface of liquid; return to the pot. 5. Stir the shredded oxtails and any accumulated juices and beans into the pot. Using the highest sauté function, cook until the soup is heated through, about 5 minutes. Stir in the vinegar and parsley and season with the salt and pepper to taste. Serve, passing preserved lemon separately.

Per Serving: Calories 420; Fat 22.8g; Sodium 540mg; Carbs 21.5g; Fiber 5.8g; Sugar 6.7g; Protein 32.4g

Greek Chicken Soup with Cauliflower Rice and Artichokes

Prep Time: 10 minutes | Cook Time: 15 minutes | Serves: 4

4 cups chicken stock

2 cups riced cauliflower, divided

2 large egg yolks

¼ cup freshly squeezed lemon juice (about 2 lemons)

¾ cup extra-virgin olive oil, divided

8 ounces cooked chicken, coarsely chopped

1 (13.75-ounce) can artichoke hearts, drained and quartered

¼ cup chopped fresh dill

1. Heat the stock in a large saucepan over medium heat until it reaches a gentle boil. Lower the heat to a simmer and cover the pan. 2. Carefully ladle 1 cup of the hot stock into a blender or food processor. Add ½ cup raw riced cauliflower, the egg yolks, and lemon juice and purée. While the processor or blender is running, stream in ½ cup olive oil and blend until smooth. 3. Whisking constantly, pour the purée into the simmering stock until well blended together and smooth. Add the chicken and artichokes and simmer until thickened slightly, 8 to 10 minutes. Stir in the dill and remaining 1½ cups riced cauliflower. 4. Serve warm, drizzled with the remaining ¼ cup olive oil.

Per Serving: Calories 290; Fat 22.6g; Sodium 490mg; Carbs 12.8g; Fiber 4.4g; Sugar 2.5g; Protein 13.8g

Savory Vegetable and Chickpea Stew

Prep Time: 25 minutes | Cook Time: 30 minutes | Serves: 6-8

¼ cup extra-virgin olive oil, plus extra for drizzling

2 red bell peppers, stemmed, seeded, and cut into 1-inch pieces

1 onion, chopped fine

½ teaspoon table salt

½ teaspoon pepper

1½ tablespoons baharat

4 garlic cloves, minced

1 tablespoon tomato paste

4 cups vegetable or chicken broth

1 (28-ounce) can whole peeled tomatoes, drained with juice reserved, chopped

1 pound Yukon Gold potatoes, peeled and cut into ½-inch pieces

2 zucchinis, quartered lengthwise and sliced 1 inch thick

1 (15-ounce) can chickpeas, rinsed

⅓ cup chopped fresh mint

1. Using the highest sauté function, heat the oil in the instant pot until shimmering. Add the bell pepper, onion, salt, and pepper and cook until the vegetables are softened and lightly browned, 5 to 7 minutes. Stir in the baharat, garlic, and tomato paste and cook until fragrant, about 1 minute. Stir in the broth and tomatoes and reserved juice, scraping up any browned bits, then stir in the potatoes. 2. Lock the lid in place and close the pressure release valve. Set to the high pressure cook function and cook for 9 minutes. Turn off the instant pot and quickly release pressure. Carefully remove the lid, ensuring the steam escapes away from you. 3. Stir the zucchini and chickpeas into the stew and cook, Using the highest sauté function, until the zucchini is tender, 10 to 15 minutes. Turn off the multicooker. Season with the salt and pepper to taste. Drizzle individual portions with the extra oil, and sprinkle with the mint before serving.

Per Serving: Calories 165; Fat 2.11g; Sodium 929mg; Carbs 31.95g; Fiber 7.3g; Sugar 10.37g; Protein 7.28g

Lamb Shanks Stew with Carrots

Prep Time: 10 minutes | Cook Time: 2 hours | Serves: 4-6

3 tablespoons extra-virgin olive oil

6 lamb shanks, trimmed

1 large onion, chopped

3 carrots, chopped

1 (15-ounce) can diced tomatoes

6 cups water

3 bay leaves

1 teaspoon salt

1. Place a large pot with a lid or Dutch oven over high heat and add the olive oil and lamb shanks. Brown on each side, about 8 minutes total. 2. Put the shanks onto a plate and add the onion and carrots to the same pot; cook for 5 minutes. 3. Add the tomatoes, water, bay leaves, and salt. Stir to combine. Add the lamb shanks back to the pot and bring to a simmer. 4. Turn the heat down to low and cover the pot. Let the shanks cook for 1 hour and 30 minutes. Remove the cover and let cook for another 20 minutes. 5. Remove the bay leaves from the pot and spoon the lamb shanks and sauce onto a serving dish. Serve warm with brown rice.

Per Serving: Calories 391; Fat 17.02g; Sodium 787mg; Carbs 9.7g; Fiber 3.3g; Sugar 5.3g; Protein 51.42g

Homemade Golden Vegetable Broth

Prep Time: 25 minutes | Cook Time: 1 hour 15 minutes | Serves: 6-8

1 tablespoon vegetable oil

3 onions, chopped

4 scallions, chopped

2 carrots, peeled and chopped

2 celery ribs, chopped

15 garlic cloves, smashed and peeled

12 cups water, divided

½ head cauliflower (1 pound), cored and cut into 1-inch pieces

1 tomato, cored and chopped

8 sprigs fresh thyme

1 teaspoon peppercorns

½ teaspoon table salt

3 bay leaves

1. Using the highest sauté function, heat the oil in the instant pot until shimmering. Add the onions, scallions, carrots, celery, and garlic and cook until the vegetables are softened and lightly browned, about 15 minutes. Pour in 1 cup water and stir, scraping up any browned bits. Then stir in the remaining 11 cups water, cauliflower, tomato, thyme sprigs, peppercorns, salt, and bay leaves. 2. Lock the lid in place and close the pressure release valve. Set to the high pressure cook function and cook for 1 hour. Turn off the instant pot and let pressure release naturally for 15 minutes. Quick-release any remaining pressure, then carefully remove the lid, ensuring the steam escapes away from you. 3. Strain the broth through a fine-mesh strainer into a large container, without pressing on solids; discard solids. (Broth can be refrigerated for up to 4 days or frozen for up to 2 months.)

Per Serving: Calories 85; Fat 2.73g; Sodium 252mg; Carbs 14.38g; Fiber 3.8g; Sugar 5.12g; Protein 2.68g

Gigante Bean Soup with Celery and Olives

Prep Time: 30 minutes | Cook Time: 12 minutes | Serves: 6-8

1½ tablespoons table salt, for brining

1 pound (2½ cups) dried gigante beans, picked over and rinsed

2 tablespoons extra-virgin olive oil, plus extra for drizzling

5 celery ribs, cut into ½-inch pieces, plus ½ cup leaves, minced

1 onion, chopped

½ teaspoon table salt

4 garlic cloves, minced

4 cups vegetable or chicken broth

4 cups water

2 bay leaves

½ cup pitted Kalamata olives, chopped

2 tablespoons minced fresh marjoram or oregano

Lemon wedges

1. Dissolve 1½ tablespoons salt in 2 quarts cold water in a large container. Add the beans and soak at room temperature for at least 8 hours or up to 24 hours. Drain and rinse well. 2. Using the highest sauté function, heat the oil in the instant pot until shimmering. Add the celery pieces, onion, and ½ teaspoon salt and cook until the vegetables are softened, about 5 minutes. Stir in the garlic and cook until fragrant, about 30 seconds. Stir in the broth, water, beans, and bay leaves. 3. Lock the lid in place and close the pressure release valve. Set to the high pressure cook function and cook for 6 minutes. Turn off the instant pot and let pressure release naturally for 15 minutes. Quick-release any remaining pressure, then carefully remove the lid, ensuring the steam escapes away from you. 4. Combine the celery leaves, olives, and marjoram in the bowl. Discard bay leaves. Season the soup with the salt and pepper to taste. Top individual portions with celery-olive mixture and drizzle with the extra oil. Serve with the lemon wedges.

Per Serving: Calories 290; Fat 8.5g; Sodium 550mg; Carbs 41g; Fiber 9g; Sugar 3.5g; Protein 12g

Chapter 9 Salad Recipes

Salmon and Avocado Poke Bowl

Prep Time: 15 minutes | Cook Time: 0 minute | Serves: 1

160g (5¾oz) very fresh salmon or yellowfin tuna, cut into 1.5cm (⅝in) dice

2 spring onions, finely chopped

A small handful of coriander, tough stems removed

½ avocado, cut into 1.5cm (⅝in) dice

1 tablespoon toasted black or white sesame seeds

¼–½ red chilli, very finely diced

For the Tamari Dressing:

½ teaspoon wasabi paste or English mustard

Juice of ½ lime

2 tablespoons tamari or dark or light soy sauce

1 teaspoon toasted sesame oil

1 teaspoon finely grated fresh ginger

1. Combine the wasabi, lime juice, oil, tamari, and ginger in a bowl. Adjust the flavors to suit your taste – it should have bite from the wasabi and sourness from the lime. It won't look like a lot, but it is just to coat the fish and avocado, not to swamp it.
2. Combine the salmon, spring onions and coriander in a bowl. Pour the dressing over the top, add the avocado and gently stir to combine. Scatter over sesame seeds and chilli and serve straight away.

Per Serving: Calories 475; Fat 24.28g; Sodium 2139mg; Carbs 19.93g; Fiber 10.7g; Sugar 3.91g; Protein 47.79g

Classic Tabbouleh Salad

Prep Time: 30 minutes | Cook Time: 0 minute | Serves: 8

1 cup bulgur wheat, grind

4 cups Italian parsley, finely chopped

2 cups ripe tomato, finely diced

1 cup green onion, finely chopped

½ cup lemon juice

½ cup extra-virgin olive oil

1½ teaspoons salt

1 teaspoon dried mint

1. Before you chop the vegetables, put the bulgur in a small bowl. Rinse with water, drain, and let stand in the bowl while you prepare the other ingredients. 2. Put the parsley, green onion, tomatoes, and bulgur into a large bowl. 3. In a small bowl, whisk together the lemon juice, salt, olive oil, and mint. 4. Pour the dressing over the tomato, onion, and bulgur mixture, tossing everything together. Add additional salt to taste. Serve immediately or store in the fridge for up to 2 days.

Per Serving: Calories 203; Fat 14.13g; Sodium 460mg; Carbs 18.22g; Fiber 3.8g; Sugar 2.04g; Protein 3.52g

Mediterranean Quinoa & Garbanzo Salad

Prep Time: 10 minutes | Cook Time: 30 minutes | Serves: 8

4 cups water

2 cups red or yellow quinoa

2 teaspoons salt, divided

1 cup thinly sliced onions (red or white)

1 (16-ounce) can garbanzo beans, rinsed and drained

⅓ cup extra-virgin olive oil

¼ cup lemon juice

1 teaspoon freshly ground black pepper

1. In a 3-quart pot over medium heat, bring the water to a boil. 2. Add the quinoa and 1 teaspoon of salt to the pot. Stir, cover, and cook over low heat for 15 to 20 minutes. 3. Turn off the heat, fluff the quinoa with a fork, cover again, and let sit for 5 to 10 more minutes. 4. Put the cooked quinoa, onions, and garbanzo beans in a large bowl. 5. In a separate small bowl, whisk together the olive oil, lemon juice, remaining 1 teaspoon of salt, and black pepper. 6. Pour the dressing over the quinoa mixture and gently toss everything together. Serve warm or cold.

Per Serving: Calories 310; Fat 11.79g; Sodium 588mg; Carbs 41.28g; Fiber 7.3g; Sugar 0.8g; Protein 10.94g

Sugar Snap Pea and Barley Salad

Prep Time: 10 minutes | Cook Time: 15 minutes | Serves: 4

2 cups water

1 cup quick-cooking barley

2 cups sugar snap pea pods

Small bunch flat-leaf parsley, chopped

½ small red onion, diced

2 tablespoons olive oil

Juice of 1 lemon

Sea salt and freshly ground pepper, to taste

1. Bring water to boil in a saucepan. Stir in the barley and cover. 2. Simmer for 10 minutes until all water is absorbed, and then let stand about 5 minutes covered. 3. Rinse the barley under cold water and combine it with the peas, parsley, olive oil, onion, and lemon juice. 4. Season with the sea salt and freshly ground pepper to taste.

Per Serving: Calories 277; Fat 7.69g; Sodium 308mg; Carbs 46.64g; Fiber 10.7g; Sugar 1.18g; Protein 7.5g

Mediterranean Style Egg Salad

Prep Time: 25 minutes | Cook Time: 0 minute | Serves: 4

4 large hard-boiled eggs, peeled and chopped

2 medium Roma tomatoes, chopped

1 medium avocado, peeled, pitted, and chopped

⅓ cup sliced black olives

2 tablespoons finely minced red onion

2 tablespoons extra-virgin olive oil

1 tablespoon freshly squeezed lemon juice

¼ teaspoon salt

¼ teaspoon freshly ground black pepper

¼ cup chopped fresh parsley, for garnish (optional)

1. In a large bowl, combine the eggs, tomatoes, avocado, olives, onion, olive oil, lemon juice, salt, and pepper. Mix well. Garnish with the parsley (if using). Serve right away or chill first. 2. Refrigerate any leftovers in an airtight container for up to 5 days.

Per Serving: Calories 233; Fat 19.6g; Sodium 217mg; Carbs 8.31g; Fiber 4.4g; Sugar 2.85g; Protein 8.03g

Tasty Shrimp Cobb Salad

Prep Time: 15 minutes | Cook Time: 5 minutes | Serves: 4

2 tablespoons freshly squeezed lemon juice

2 tablespoons extra-virgin olive oil, divided

½ teaspoon Dijon mustard

½ teaspoon paprika

¼ teaspoon salt

¼ teaspoon freshly ground black pepper

1 pound large shrimp, peeled and deveined

6 cups chopped romaine lettuce

2 large hard-boiled eggs, peeled and chopped

1 cup frozen petite corn kernels, thawed

1 medium avocado, peeled, pitted, and chopped

1 small English cucumber, halved and sliced

1. In a small bowl, whisk together the lemon juice, 1½ tablespoons of olive oil, mustard, salt, paprika, and pepper. Set aside. 2. In a large skillet, heat the remaining ½ tablespoon of olive oil over medium heat. Add the shrimp and cook for 2 minutes on each side, or until pink and cooked through. 3. Assemble the salad by topping the lettuce with rows of eggs, corn, avocado, cucumber, and cooked shrimp. Drizzle with the dressing and toss everything just before serving.

Per Serving: Calories 321; Fat 18.71g; Sodium 836mg; Carbs 17.9g; Fiber 6g; Sugar 2.89g; Protein 21.85g

Tomato and Pepper Salad

Prep Time: 10 minutes | Cook Time: 0 minute | Serves: 6

3 large yellow peppers

¼ cup olive oil

1 small bunch fresh basil leaves

2 cloves garlic, minced

4 large tomatoes, seeded and diced

Sea salt and freshly ground pepper, to taste

1. Preheat a broiler to high heat and broil the peppers until blackened on all sides. 2. Remove from heat and place in a paper bag. Seal and allow the peppers to cool. 3. Once cooled, peel the skins off the peppers, then seed and chop them. 4. Add half of the peppers to a food processor along with the olive oil, basil, and garlic, and pulse several times to make the dressing. 5. Combine the rest of the peppers with the tomatoes and toss with the dressing. 5. Season the salad with the sea salt and freshly ground pepper. Allow the salad to come to room temperature before serving.

Per Serving: Calories 98; Fat 7.3g; Sodium 4mg; Carbs 7.1g; Fiber 2.1g; Sugar 4.5g; Protein 1.3g

Carrot, Cabbage, and Chickpea Salad

Prep Time: 10 minutes | Cook Time: 0 minute | Serves: 2

100g (3½oz) carrots, scrubbed and coarsely grated

200g (7oz) red or white cabbage

240g (8½oz) cooked or canned chickpeas, black, borlotti or cannellini beans, drained

1 green chilli or a pinch of chilli flakes

A small handful of coriander or flat-leaf parsley, roughly

chopped

1 tablespoon extra-virgin olive oil

Juice of ½ lemon or a splash of cider vinegar

½ teaspoon ground cumin

½ teaspoon black onion (nigella) seeds

For the Tahini Dressing:

2 tablespoons tahini

Juice of ½ lemon or a splash of cider vinegar

Salt and freshly ground black pepper

To Serve (Optional):

4 soft-boiled eggs, halved

1 teaspoon sesame seeds

1. Mix together the dressing ingredients and add 2 tablespoons of water to dilute to a creamy consistency. Season to taste with the extra lemon juice, salt, and pepper. Use straight away or keep in the fridge for up to 3 days. 2. Mix together all the salad ingredients in a large bowl. Divide between 2 salad bowls, splash over the dressing and serve.

Per Serving: Calories 547; Fat 30.21g; Sodium 1087mg; Carbs 47.25g; Fiber 13.6g; Sugar 13.01g; Protein 26.53g

Sardine Cannellini Bean Salad

Prep Time: 10 minutes | Cook Time: 0 minute | Serves: 4

1 red onion, thinly sliced into half-moons

10 cherry tomatoes, halved

2 celery sticks, cut finely on the diagonal, plus a small handful of celery leaves, to garnish

1 small yellow pepper, cut into thin strips

240g (8½oz) cooked or canned cannellini or borlotti beans, drained

1 tablespoon fresh oregano leaves or ½ teaspoon dried oregano

A little finely chopped red chilli, to taste, or ¼ teaspoon chilli flakes

2 tablespoons red wine vinegar

5 tablespoons extra virgin olive oil

2 x 120g (4½oz) cans sardines in olive oil, drained (170g/6oz net weight)

A small handful of basil leaves

Salt and freshly ground black pepper

1. Put the sliced onions in a bowl of cold water and leave to soak for 10 minutes. (This will make them less potent.) Drain well. 2. Put the tomatoes, celery, beans, oregano, pepper, and chilli in a large bowl, add the onions and mix with a large spoon. Splash over the vinegar and 4 tablespoons of the oil, season with the salt and pepper and stir again. 3. Break the sardines into the salad. Stir gently to combine, without flaking the fish. Taste and add more seasoning or chilli as necessary. (At this point, before adding the basil, the salad will keep well in an airtight container in the fridge for a couple of days.) 4. To serve, arrange the salad on a large plate. Tear over the basil and celery leaves and drizzle over the remaining olive oil.

Per Serving: Calories 332; Fat 22.25g; Sodium 432mg; Carbs 17.1g; Fiber 6.3g; Sugar 1.37g; Protein 16.54g

Green Salad with Vinaigrette

Prep Time: 10 minutes | Cook Time: 0 minute | Serves: 4

400g (14oz) green salad leaves, such as round lettuce, chicory, radicchio, rocket and/or watercress

For the Vinaigrette:

1 tablespoon red wine vinegar

4 tablespoons extra virgin olive oil

1 teaspoon Dijon mustard

Salt and freshly ground black pepper

1. Put the vinaigrette ingredients into a jar with a lid and shake to combine. Season to taste. 2. Toss the green salad leaves in the dressing just before serving.

Per Serving: Calories 134; Fat 13.77g; Sodium 310mg; Carbs 2.49g; Fiber 1.2g; Sugar 0.95g; Protein 1.42g

Perfect Shrimp Ceviche Salad

Prep Time: 15 minutes | Cook Time: 0 minute | Serves: 4

1 pound fresh shrimp, peeled and deveined

1 small red or yellow bell pepper, cut into ½-inch chunks

½ English cucumber, peeled and cut into ½-inch chunks

½ small red onion, cut into thin slivers

¼ cup chopped fresh cilantro or flat-leaf Italian parsley

⅓ cup freshly squeezed lime juice

2 tablespoons freshly squeezed lemon juice

2 tablespoons freshly squeezed clementine juice or orange juice

½ cup extra-virgin olive oil

1 teaspoon salt

½ teaspoon freshly ground black pepper

2 ripe avocados, peeled, pitted, and cut into ½-inch chunks

1. Cut the shrimp in half lengthwise. In a large glass bowl, combine the shrimp, bell pepper, onion, cucumber, and cilantro. 2. In a small bowl, whisk together the lime, lemon, and clementine juices, salt, olive oil, and pepper. Pour the mixture over the shrimp and veggies and toss to coat. Cover and refrigerate for at least 2 hours, or up to 8 hours. Give the mixture a toss every 30 minutes for the first 2 hours to make sure all the shrimp "cook" in the juices. 3. Add the cut avocado just before serving and toss to combine.

Per Serving: Calories 296; Fat 17.16g; Sodium 728mg; Carbs 14.53g; Fiber 7.6g; Sugar 3.16g; Protein 25.58g

Bulgur Salad with Carrots and Almonds

Prep Time: 10 minutes | Cook Time: 0 minute | Serves: 8

1½ cups medium-grind bulgur, rinsed

1 cup water

6 tablespoons lemon juice (2 lemons)

Salt and pepper

⅓ cup extra-virgin olive oil

½ teaspoon ground cumin

⅛ teaspoon cayenne pepper

4 carrots, peeled and shredded

3 scallions, sliced thin

½ cup sliced almonds, toasted

⅓ cup chopped fresh mint

⅓ cup chopped fresh cilantro

1. Combine the bulgur, water, ¼ cup lemon juice, and ¼ teaspoon salt in a bowl. Cover and let sit at room temperature until the grains are softened and liquid is fully absorbed, about 1½ hours. 2. Whisk the remaining 2 tablespoons lemon juice, oil, cayenne, cumin, and ¼ teaspoon salt together in a large bowl. Add the bulgur, carrots, almonds, mint, scallions, and cilantro and gently toss to combine. Season with the pepper to taste. Serve.

Per Serving: Calories 221; Fat 12.3g; Sodium 174mg; Carbs 25.63g; Fiber 5.2g; Sugar 2.24g; Protein 4.97g

Tomato Tabbouleh Salad

Prep Time: 10 minutes | Cook Time: 0 minute | Serves: 4

3 tomatoes, cored and cut into ½-inch pieces
Salt and pepper
½ cup medium-grind bulgur, rinsed
¼ cup lemon juice (2 lemons)
6 tablespoons extra-virgin olive oil

⅛ teaspoon cayenne pepper
1½ cups minced fresh parsley
½ cup minced fresh mint
2 scallions, sliced thin

1. Toss the tomatoes with ¼ teaspoon salt in a fine-mesh strainer set over a bowl and let drain, tossing occasionally, for 30 minutes; reserve 2 tablespoons drained tomato juice. Combine the bulgur, 2 tablespoons lemon juice, and reserved tomato juice in a bowl and let sit until the grains begin to soften, 30 to 40 minutes. 2. Whisk the remaining 2 tablespoons lemon juice, cayenne, oil, and ¼ teaspoon salt together in a large bowl. Add the tomatoes, bulgur, mint, parsley, and scallions and gently toss to combine. Cover and allow to sit at room temperature until flavors have melded and grains are softened, about 1 hour. Before serving, toss the salad to recombine and season with pepper to taste.
Per Serving: Calories 220; Fat 14g; Sodium 150mg; Carbs 22g; Fiber 5g; Sugar 4g; Protein 3g

Kale Tomato Salad

Prep Time: 10 minutes | Cook Time: 5 minutes | Serves: 4

2 heads kale
1+ tablespoon olive oil
2 cloves garlic, minced

1 cup cherry tomatoes, sliced
Sea salt and freshly ground pepper, to taste
Juice of 1 lemon

1. Rinse and dry kale. 2. Tear the kale into bite-sized pieces. 3. Heat 1 tablespoon of the olive oil in a large skillet, add the garlic, and cook for 1 minute. 4. Then add the kale and cook just until wilted. 5. Then add the tomatoes and cook until tomatoes are softened. 6. Remove from heat. Place the tomatoes and kale in a bowl, and season with the sea salt and freshly ground pepper. Drizzle with the remaining olive oil and lemon juice, serve, and enjoy.
Per Serving: Calories 169; Fat 7.31g; Sodium 379mg; Carbs 22.99g; Fiber 8.8g; Sugar 6.43g; Protein 10.23g

Mediterranean Potato Salad

Prep Time: 10 minutes | Cook Time: 20 minutes | Serves: 6

2 pounds Yukon Gold baby potatoes, cut into 1-inch cubes

3 tablespoons freshly squeezed lemon juice (from about 1 medium lemon)

3 tablespoons extra-virgin olive oil

1 tablespoon olive brine

¼ teaspoon kosher or sea salt

1 (2.25-ounce) can sliced olives (about ½ cup)

1 cup sliced celery (about 2 stalks) or fennel

2 tablespoons chopped fresh oregano

2 tablespoons torn fresh mint

1. In a medium saucepan, cover the potatoes with cold water until the waterline is one inch above the potatoes. Set over high heat, bring the potatoes to a boil, then turn down the heat to medium-low. Simmer for 12 to 15 minutes, until the potatoes are just fork tender. 2. While the potatoes are cooking, in a small bowl, whisk together the lemon juice, olive brine, oil, and salt. 3. Drain the potatoes in a colander and transfer to a serving bowl. Immediately pour about 3 tablespoons of the dressing over the potatoes. Gently mix in the olives and celery. 4. Before serving, gently mix in the oregano, mint, and the remaining dressing.
Per Serving: Calories 192; Fat 7.78g; Sodium 171mg; Carbs 28.79g; Fiber 4.2g; Sugar 1.96g; Protein 3.38g

Freekeh, Chickpea, and Herb Salad

Prep Time: 15 minutes | Cook Time: 10 minutes | Serves: 4-6

1 (15-ounce) can chickpeas, rinsed and drained

1 cup cooked freekeh

1 cup thinly sliced celery

1 bunch scallions, both white and green parts, finely chopped

½ cup chopped fresh flat-leaf parsley

¼ cup chopped fresh mint

3 tablespoons chopped celery leaves

½ teaspoon kosher salt

⅓ cup extra-virgin olive oil

¼ cup freshly squeezed lemon juice

¼ teaspoon cumin seeds

1 teaspoon garlic powder

1. In a large bowl, combine the chickpeas, freekeh, celery, scallions, mint, celery leaves, parsley, and salt and toss lightly. 2. In a small bowl, whisk together the olive oil, cumin seeds, lemon juice, and garlic powder. Once combined, add to freekeh salad.
Per Serving: Calories 254; Fat 16g; Sodium 386mg; Carbs 24.44g; Fiber 5.8g; Sugar 3.31g; Protein 5.22g

Arugula and Artichoke Salad

Prep Time: 20 minutes | Cook Time: 0 minute | Serves: 6

4 tablespoons olive oil

2 tablespoons balsamic vinegar

1 teaspoon Dijon mustard

1 clove garlic, minced

6 cups baby arugula leaves

6 oil-packed artichoke hearts, sliced

6 low-salt olives, pitted and chopped

1 cup cherry tomatoes, sliced in half

4 fresh basil leaves, thinly sliced

1. Make the dressing by whisking together the olive oil, vinegar, Dijon, and garlic until you have a smooth emulsion. Set aside. 2. Toss the arugula, artichokes, olives, and tomatoes together. 3. Drizzle the salad with the dressing, garnish with the fresh basil, and serve.

Per Serving: Calories 129; Fat 11.98g; Sodium 74mg; Carbs 5.14g; Fiber 2.7g; Sugar 1.56g; Protein 11.98g

Lemon Pepper Tuna Arugula Salad

Prep Time: 5 minutes | Cook Time: 0 minute | Serves: 4

2 (5-ounce) cans chunk light tuna packed in water, drained

¼ cup plain nonfat Greek yogurt

1 medium shallot, finely chopped

2 tablespoons freshly squeezed lemon juice

2 teaspoons grated lemon zest

½ teaspoon freshly ground black pepper

4 cups arugula

1. In a medium bowl, combine the tuna, yogurt, shallot, lemon zest, lemon juice, and pepper until mixed. 2. Serve the salad over the arugula. 3. Refrigerate any leftovers in an airtight container for up to 5 days.

Per Serving: Calories 74; Fat 0.87g; Sodium 183mg; Carbs 2.27g; Fiber 0.5g; Sugar 1.07g; Protein 15.06g

Spinach Tomato Salad

Prep Time: 10 minutes | Cook Time: 5 minutes | Serves: 4

1 large ripe tomato

1 medium red onion

½ teaspoon fresh lemon zest

3 tablespoons balsamic vinegar

¼ cup extra-virgin olive oil

½ teaspoon salt

1 pound baby spinach, washed, stems removed

1. Dice the tomato into ¼-inch pieces and slice the onion into long slivers. 2. In a small bowl, whisk together the lemon zest, balsamic vinegar, olive oil, and salt. 3. Put the spinach, tomatoes, and onions in a large bowl. Add the dressing to the salad and lightly toss to coat.

Per Serving: Calories 175; Fat 14.06g; Sodium 387mg; Carbs 10.54g; Fiber 3.5g; Sugar 4.65g; Protein 4.01g

Conclusion

Congratulations on taking the first steps toward a healthier, happier you! The Zero Point Weight Loss Cookbook for Beginners is more than just a collection of recipes—it's a gateway to a sustainable and joyful approach to eating. As you've seen throughout this book, zero point foods are about abundance, not restriction. They empower you to nourish your body with delicious meals while still achieving your weight loss goals.

By now, you've discovered the incredible diversity of recipes in this cookbook. From energizing breakfasts to hearty dinners, the options are endless. This variety ensures that you'll never grow bored or feel deprived, even on the busiest days. These recipes are designed to fit seamlessly into your lifestyle, making it easier than ever to stay on track.

The journey doesn't end here. Remember, sustainable weight loss is about creating habits you can maintain for life. Use the meal plans, cooking tips, and insights in this book as tools to guide you. Experiment with new ingredients, try different recipes, and don't be afraid to make these meals your own. The key is to enjoy the process and celebrate the small wins along the way.

We hope this cookbook has inspired you to see healthy eating in a new light—one where food is both your fuel and your joy. Whether you're cooking for yourself, your family, or friends, these meals will leave everyone feeling satisfied and nourished.

Thank you for letting us be part of your journey. Here's to achieving your goals, feeling your best, and embracing the delicious simplicity of zero point eating.

Appendix 1 Measurement Conversion Chart

VOLUME EQUIVALENTS (LIQUID)

US STANDARD	US STANDARD (OUNCES)	METRIC (APPROXIMATE)
2 tablespoons	1 fl.oz	30 mL
¼ cup	2 fl.oz	60 mL
½ cup	4 fl.oz	120 mL
1 cup	8 fl.oz	240 mL
1½ cup	12 fl.oz	355 mL
2 cups or 1 pint	16 fl.oz	475 mL
4 cups or 1 quart	32 fl.oz	1 L
1 gallon	128 fl.oz	4 L

VOLUME EQUIVALENTS (DRY)

US STANDARD	METRIC (APPROXIMATE)
⅛ teaspoon	0.5 mL
¼ teaspoon	1 mL
½ teaspoon	2 mL
¾ teaspoon	4 mL
1 teaspoon	5 mL
1 tablespoon	15 mL
¼ cup	59 mL
½ cup	118 mL
¾ cup	177 mL
1 cup	235 mL
2 cups	475 mL
3 cups	700 mL
4 cups	1 L

TEMPERATURES EQUIVALENTS

FAHRENHEIT(F)	CELSIUS(C) (APPROXIMATE)
225 °F	107 °C
250 °F	120 °C
275 °F	135 °C
300 °F	150 °C
325 °F	160 °C
350 °F	180 °C
375 °F	190 °C
400 °F	205 °C
425 °F	220 °C
450 °F	235 °C
475 °F	245 °C
500 °F	260 °C

WEIGHT EQUIVALENTS

US STANDARD	METRIC (APPROXINATE)
1 ounce	28 g
2 ounces	57 g
5 ounces	142 g
10 ounces	284 g
15 ounces	425 g
16 ounces (1 pound)	455 g
1.5pounds	680 g
2pounds	907 g

Appendix 2 Recipes Index

Made in the USA
Monee, IL
09 January 2025